T0147176

MAKE LUCK HAPPEN

Create the Effective, Consistently Lucky Person

Who Practices Leadership through Structured Problem-Solving

Rico Vidas, JD, Leadership Consultant

WESTBOW
PRESS®
A DIVISION OF THOMAS NELSON
& ZONDERVAN

WestBow Press books may be ordered through booksellers or by contacting:

WestBow Press
A Division of Thomas Nelson & Zondervan
1663 Liberty Drive
Bloomington, IN 47403
www.westbowpress.com
1 (866) 928-1240

Scripture quotations marked KJV are taken from the King James Version.

Scripture quotations marked DRA are taken from the Douay-Rheims Bible, American edition.

ISBN: 978-1-9736-7628-7 (sc)
ISBN: 978-1-9736-7630-0 (hc)
ISBN: 978-1-9736-7629-4 (e)

Library of Congress Control Number: 2019915316

Print information available on the last page.

WestBow Press rev. date: 10/4/2019

Do you want, or need, to be a leader? There is a great need for truly effective leaders.

This book prepares the reader to use the protocols for problem-solving to create the effective, consistently lucky person who can lead by learning how to excel during the heat of battle, defeat extreme narcissism, and be at their finest during the darkest crisis.

After setting forth the relevant how and why of leadership, part 2 winds up with lessons for life as an effective person.

These are case studies that illustrate leadership in action against what, at the time, seem impossible odds.

Contents

Preface

Few people who know the author would disagree with his being described as an experienced, effective problem solver, but what he aspires to be is an effective poverty warrior, an economic emancipator for people who feel economically trapped, working in drudgery, from paycheck to paycheck, just to survive, with no resources for self-actualization, diversions, or family development and growth. This book is dedicated to them.

This is a book designed to provide tools, strategies, and procedures to assist in empowering the economically trapped, members of their family, students, and other beneficiaries, to change their reality for the better and forever.

We start with leadership as exercised by people who are effective because they are experienced at solving difficult problems. This is the first step in empowering the escape of those who are economically depressed and feel trapped.

We wind up with lessons for life as an effective person. Lessons 1 through 9 provide case studies that illustrate leadership and the use of protocols for problem-solving in action against what many times seem to be impossible odds.

Introduction

While learning the protocols of problems-solving and how to be consistently lucky, I came to value people with experience, to seek the advice of those who had been there before and who could provide me with the lessons learned from their experience. Trying now to explain why this is so, the underlying reasons and the foundation upon which this book is based became clear.

As will be emphasized throughout this treatise, the key to solving problems and being lucky is the ability to *recognize* problems and opportunities. You cannot solve a problem unless you first recognize that there is a problem. Similarly, statistically, everyone encounters opportunities, but the issue is whether or not one is sufficiently prepared to recognize the opportunity and seize it.

How many opportunities have passed us by that we never recognized? When one exploits their preparedness by recognizing and seizing an opportunity, others tend to describe them as being lucky. The person who worked hard to be prepared will sometimes answer, "Yeah, luck spelled w-o-r-k." Many people have noticed that the harder they work, the luckier they get.

The key to recognition is experience. This is demonstrated by the following analysis:

- A unit of meaning is the relationship between a thing and another thing or idea.
- The ability to recognize is the ability to see these units of meaning, the relationships and the connections between different things and ideas.

- The more things or ideas a person has experienced, the more connections and relationships that can be recognized.
- If a person has the experience of seeing a dark cloud and the rain that comes from it, the next time that person sees a dark cloud, they recognize the possibility that rain may be forthcoming.
- The dark cloud is recognized as a potential for rain because of the person's previous experience.
- The more experience, the more dark clouds that have been encountered, the greater the capability of recognizing their meaning.
- Experience is important because it generally means that there is a statistical probability that more things or ideas have been encountered, and this creates a greater ability to recognize problems and opportunities.
- The ability to recognize is the key to solving problems and the key to seizing opportunities.
- Once a problem is recognized, the problem-solving protocols can be initiated.
- An opportunity cannot be seized unless it has first been recognized and its meaning and potential identified.

A central premise of this book is that a wide base of experience enables one to recognize problems and opportunities where less experienced individuals are blind. It is this recognition that invokes the power to use problem-solving protocols and see opportunities that can be seized to create good fortune. Experience provides the eyes for managing problems and seizing opportunities.

The influential book *Leading Change* by Professor Kotter states that the guiding group of planners seeking change is more effective if it includes individuals from all levels of the issue involved in the change process. You need the executive viewpoint, but you also need the technicians, the mechanics, even the maintenance people to be involved. It is necessary to have a representative from each relevant level, whose personal experience at their level will provide insights and knowledge to which the others are blind.

To be effective, the experience and recognition capabilities of all should be integrated into the process so that there can be greater recognition of the forces at work and the opportunities available.

The author of this treatise has spent a lifetime in this practice. This book is an attempt to communicate the relevant knowledge that he has accumulated.

The author's experience is unusually varied and typically at a high decision-making level. It covers politics where he was a delegate to a national presidential nominating convention and served as a planning commissioner for a major American city.

He has been a principal in industrial ventures such as mining, where he secured the rights to a mine that had produced more than six thousand ounces of gold and in which he found new veins of gold. His construction enterprises included building classrooms and multipurpose conference halls for high school districts, and also an animal hospital for a municipal zoo. He has drilled oil wells in Tennessee and experimented with techniques for the recovery of nonproducing older wells.

The experience includes financial products where he founded an insurance agency that developed new approaches to retirement plans. He engaged in small and minority business development pursuant to government contracts. This included providing minority businesses with support services paid for by government programs. He programed a computer accounting system before the development of Quicken and QuickBooks. He has engaged in the successful development of numerous real estate housing, commercial, and industrial projects and has invented methods of financing to develop low-income housing. He served as chairman of the board of a national bank and spent two decades in the practice of law.

He has developed inventions and assisted others in bringing new technologies to market. He has developed procedures and protocols for the installation of portable housing infrastructure products where there are no utilities available. He has also served as a professor of history and chairman of an academic department of a state university. He has engaged in private investment banking, developed real estate syndications, and creating and published financial securities private placement memorandum documents and offering circulars.

Because of this long and varied, hands-on background in creating new approaches to law, finance, construction and development, insurance, education, and new technologies, the author sees meaning, problems to be solved, and opportunities for good fortune almost everywhere. For him, the key now is focusing on that which is important today and in the future. Part of what is important is sharing his insights and knowledge for the future good. That was the genesis for writing this book.

PART I

A Call for Effective Leadership and Good Citizenship

Good citizenship is important. Becoming an effective citizen who knows how to solve problems will inevitably lead to leadership for self, for family, and for the greater community. Good citizens who recognize the needs of their family and community will naturally be compelled to do something to solve glaring problems.

But many times, the problems are so big and appear to be so far beyond a person's resources that it appears impossible to do anything that will be effective. They can't conceive of anything they can do beyond their present ineffective activity, so they do nothing, and the problems remain. They don't know how to find a solution.

This book is about how—how to be a leader who knows how to figure out what must be done to be effective, who is willing to act to get it done, and who can persevere in the face of adversity. A key component is a learned behavior. It is perseverance that, after a decision has been made to embark upon the undertaking, compels the leader to fight on and never conceive of giving up.

It is the desire of the author that after the experience of being introduced to concepts described, preached, and advocated in this book, the reader will, with confidence, begin to overcome barriers, pursue noble goals, and discover outlets for their compassion and idealism.

It is hoped that the ideas contained herein will focus attention and efforts on the positive and better angels of our human nature to inspire others to follow their positive example. The focus needs to be to encourage, to nurture, to build, to lead by example and never, ever to criticize, tear down, or degrade others.

We define a leader as one who takes the initiative in solving a problem.

CHAPTER 1
The Protocols of Problem-Solving

Background

During the period of 1965 to 1973, I, the author, was involved in the War on Poverty and community organizing. From 1961 to 1963, I had been deeply involved in Democratic Party affairs in Southern California. A former congressman had become my mentor, and I excelled in political campaigns and interparty intrigues during the battles for control of the party between the followers of Speaker of the state assembly, "Big Daddy" Jesse Unruh and the California Democratic Council (CDC), a grass roots organization of Democratic clubs.

Depending on your loyalties, these political battles for control of the Democratic Party in Southern California were the professionals versus the amateurs (Jesse Unruh was the chief professional) or the cynical machine politicians versus the idealist believers in justice and democracy (CDC).

Numerous congressional and assembly seats were in play in the 1962 primaries, and being in the center put me in what amounted to an advanced curriculum in power politics. In this arena, more could be learned about power and politics in two years than could be accumulated in forty years as a business executive. Before I was old enough to vote, I became the head of the Assembly District Democratic Council and ran my mother for County Committee where she, as a housewife, received twelve thousand votes.

A successful winner of a congressional seat, George E. Brown Jr., agreed to sponsor me for a trip to Washington, DC, and secured an appointment by President John Kennedy to an internship at the Department of Labor, and then I was released to the congressman's Capitol Hill office.

Being in Washington, DC, during the incredible summer of 1963 was a heady experience for a nineteen-year-old Mexican American from Watts via East Los Angeles. I traveled there by Greyhound bus and returned by jet airplane. By analogy, this represented how much I grew and how big my world became that summer. Martin Luther King gave his "I Have a Dream" speech that summer about three months before President Kennedy was assassinated.

Upon return home to Los Angeles, California, I became involved in Mexican American civic affairs and was involved in the fight for control of President Lyndon Johnson's War on Poverty Program, first in Los Angeles and then in San Francisco. The community groups lost the fight for control in Los Angeles but won in San Francisco.

My entry into law school in San Francisco coincided with a struggle for control of poverty program funds. It was a classic power struggle for which I, having been tutored by the best power politicians in Southern California, was perfectly suited. It did not take long for the political experience to exhibit itself. I was elected chairman of the Economic Opportunity Council in the Mission District and served on the citywide board of directors. I became a key player in the power struggles.

But political power struggles coupled with the effort needed to win were not compatible with the effort needed to survive academically at a very difficult and famous law school. Eventually, the load was so heavy that I had to quit everything except being a full-time law student.

As law school came to end, I needed a job. An offer came in for work as a community organizer in Phoenix, Arizona. I contacted a friend who was associated with a school of social welfare at a nearby university. I was advised that I would be an excellent community organizer.

I responded that the only problem was that I had no idea what a community organizer was or what they did. I was told that they assisted communities in organizing to solve the community's problems. But first, they had to learn how. Hence, the academics had developed a guide that I called the protocols of problem-solving.

These were explained to me. When I said I wasn't sure I agreed with some of them, I was told it wasn't opinion; they had data, this is what they knew, and I should shut up and listen. I did so. This knowledge combined with my political experience and my experience as a leader made me very effective at community organization.

These protocols are a sophisticated version of trial and error, which is how most human knowledge has been gained. I have been using these protocols ever since that early experience in mobilizing communities. I now say that an individual can use them for personal goals as well.

The Protocols of Problem-Solving

There are eight elements that I refer to as protocols to problem-solving. We seldom realize that whenever we solve a problem, we go through this process. But sometimes in complex situations, it becomes necessary to analyze protocols separately. These protocols follow:

1. *Problem recognition and definition.* Before you can solve a problem, you need to recognize that you have a problem and know how to define it. What are its parts? How do they connect with one another? A key element here is the question, Who defines the problem? How it is defined is critical and will affect the solution.

   If the perceived problem is slavery, the solution may be quite different if the problem is defined by the slave owner rather than by the slave. Implications inherent in the definition will suggest the outcome. Leaders needs to make sure that the person defining the problem shares their analysis and goals.

2. *Information gathering.* Engage in research on the problem.

3. *Analysis.* Take apart the information and see how the elements connect with one another. What is the structure? Search for causes and effects.

4. *Formulation of goals.* This will require value decisions. Many times, it may require tradeoffs between two evils and having to decide which one to choose. These may be the only options available. If there are no good options and immediate action is

not necessary, the best strategy may be to do nothing and wait for better options.

Change is a fact of life, and things change with time. Sometimes, however, the consequences are such that one cannot wait and must act with insufficient knowledge and no good choices. Many times, it is better that a wrong decision be made rather than no decision.

When in a situation where immediate action is called for and the correct decision is not clearly visible, indecision will halt necessary progress and damage the potential for success. A wrong decision will expose the error, and with this new knowledge gained by trial and error, a correction leading to progress can be made. A decision acted upon, even if it is wrong, is better than no decision.

5. *Strategy.* Never worry about deciding on your strategy. The implications of combining the analysis with your goals will suggest your strategy.
6. *Implementation.* Put the strategy to work. Test it to see if it works.
7. *Feedback and evaluation from the attempted implementation.*
8. *Reformulation of goals based upon results from the above.* Now there is new information that can be added for analysis and new implications with which to adjust strategy. One needs to continually start over again from this point. Most human knowledge has come from trial and error. Use trial and error until the problem is solved.

CHAPTER 2
The Importance, Relevance, and Value of Recognition

Engaging in problem-solving enables a person to develop skills and talent at recognizing two extremely important concepts. These are problems and opportunities.

Recognizing Problems

Some problems are easy to recognize, and some stay unrecognized for centuries. Problems involving traditions and conditioning can be very difficult to recognize from the inside. These require a coach viewing from the outside and may need neurolinguistic programming analysis.

For example, during the Middle Ages, the Spanish Inquisition's reputation for cruelty was well deserved. The inquisitors did not see a problem because they believed they were doing God's work and protecting the one true faith. People may disagree in this regard, but the fact is when the Spanish arrived in Mexico, they encountered a religion that was far worse.

The Aztec church engaged in human sacrifice. The Aztec priest had the power of life and death over the populace. They chose who would be sacrificed to the Aztec gods. They drugged the victims, took them up to the top of a pyramid, and cut out their hearts. The inquisitors suddenly found themselves to be the kind, compassionate, Christian alternative.

Now the question is posed: did the Aztec common people have a problem with the Aztec church? An outsider would probably say yes, but to an insider, this situation was normal and the will of the gods. The people had been conditioned to accept the religion as normal. It was their tradition. Problems involving traditions and conditioning are extremely difficult for insiders to recognize.

Once a slave recognizes that their situation is not normal and not really the will of God, it is only then that change or escape becomes a problem to be solved. They will have finally recognized that they have a problem.

Problem recognition is a valuable skill.

CHAPTER 3
Opportunities and Luck

Recognition of opportunities is a function of education, experience, and preparation. If you have an objective and engage in problem-solving efforts, you are involved in the preparation aspect of problem-solving. This preparation develops the ability to recognize opportunities while you are seeking a solution to your problem.

When you combine this with the laws of probability, something wonderful happens. Statistics prove that, as a matter of probability, we all get opportunities. Many go right past us, and we never see them. The issue is whether or not we will be prepared enough to recognize them. We need to be sufficiently prepared to do two things:

a. We need to be prepared enough to recognize an opportunity.
b. We need to be prepared enough to seize the opportunity.

Luck is the convergence of preparation and opportunity. We all get opportunities, but will we be sufficiently prepared to seize them? If so, others will say, "Boy, are you lucky!"

What if you do not recognize any opportunities when you need them?

Among the options you can think of, consider these two actions: One is giving yourself a chance to be lucky. You can't win the lottery if you don't buy a ticket.

You can sometimes put yourself in proximity to be lucky. My grandfather used to say, "You don't know what you can do until you try." When the outcome is in doubt and you try anyway, you are giving yourself a chance to be lucky. What I have found is that I am lucky about 70 percent of the time. Most people tend to take for granted the times when they are lucky and complain about the 30 percent of the time when they are not lucky. It is better to forget about being unlucky and spend the time thanking God for the times he allowed you to be lucky.

An equally important action and concept is what my college football coach called playing for a break. You continue playing as hard as you can and keep your senses open while you search for an opportunity, a break.

Two Examples of Playing for a Break

1. The first time this entered my world was during a football game in college. The other side began by running all over us. We were behind 14–0 in the first quarter, and nothing we did could stop the opposing team. The coach said, "I know it looks impossible now, but if you keep playing hard, a break will come, and we need to stay in there until it does." It did. The momentum of the game changed, and we became unstoppable. That was my initiation to playing for a break. It took two hours to learn the lesson.
2. This is a more important example of playing for a break. This time it took six weeks to demonstrate the lesson.

When I started law school, I tried to follow all the good advice people gave me. Very soon I found that even if I studied twenty-four hours a day, I could not complete the assignments given. I thought that I wasn't good enough because I could not do the assignments within the time available. The stress caused me to develop a rash on my hands, and I had to take medication. I decided I would never quit, and if necessary, I would go down fighting. Never quit was built into my DNA. My parents conditioned me not to be a quitter. I was expected to be a winner, which placed great pressure and stress on me. But this also meant that I would stay in the arena, work as hard as I could, and play for a break. Then after about six weeks, I found that I could do the work. I had gotten better at it. Without realizing it, I had developed the skill. Playing for a break worked.

Now I always give myself a chance to be lucky, and I am always willing to play for a break.

Career Advice

I remember a newspaper editor who would always advise young people to find something that they like and get good at it. Be the best there ever was at what you want to do.

But how can a normal adolescent become the best? It takes hard work and lots of luck. That represents a problem we now know how to work on and attack. We also now know what luck is and how to be lucky. We start preparing as early as possible and practice to perfect our skills so that we can always recognize and seize opportunities as they pass our way while we develop as a person.

CHAPTER 4
A Reasonable Effort versus the Effort Required

Getting good at something requires effort, training, and lots and lots of practice. In high school, I wanted to be a track star, but I wasn't fast enough. Quickness, which I had, worked in football, but it did not seem to have a place on the track field. Then my father and one of my coaches advised me that I could use quickness in an event called the shot put, where you push a twelve-pound steel ball as far as possible. Generally, this event was for athletes who were bigger, heavier, and stronger than me.

However, I soon found that what others did with brute strength, I could match with technique and form. I could harness the momentum of my body weight to put additional thrust on the steel ball my arm was pushing. Developing this form took practice.

Every time I pushed the ball, I had immediate feedback on how well I was doing by the distance the ball traveled. For a long time, I wasn't doing very well at all. I started practicing and playing for a break. It got to the point that I was at the pit just at daylight with my lunch in hand, and I practiced until it was so dark I could not see. I spent an entire summer doing this, and it seemed hopeless. Then, when I least expected it, the ball sailed into new territory, farther than ever before. That season, I was league champ in the shot put for my classification.

Most people who talked to me about this felt that my effort was unreasonable and silly, that they would, and should, do only what was reasonable. For most things, maybe there is something to that. The reasonable man test is the standard for the law of negligence.

But if you want to be the best, the effort required is unreasonable.

Life requires competition, and the champions are those who are willing and able to teach themselves, to learn more, to prepare more, and then to practice and train in the amounts necessary to beat the competition. Never underestimate the heart of a champion or what they can accomplish.

When I first went out for football, I was told by almost everybody that I was too small to play football, especially with the varsity big boys. I asked my grandfather, who had been coaching me, if I was indeed too small. He answered, "If your heart is big enough, then you're big enough." By the end of the following year, I was captain of the varsity squad.

This concept can carry over to other individuals, to teams, and to business ventures and companies. Build the culture, develop the heart, work, practice, train, and then watch the champions in action. Remember that constant failure is part of the learning process and a reason why you are almost always playing for a break.

CHAPTER 5
The Strategic Importance of Perspective and Knowing One's Power Position

What is perspective? It is the ability to see situations clearly so that accurate analysis is possible.

An accurate perspective is mandatory for a leader.

A leader must be able to make an accurate analysis of their position and make decisions that will affect the lives and actions of others who are their responsibility. Bizarre decisions that turn out to be very bad are generally the result of an inadequate perspective by at least one of the responsible parties.

Power Position

It is critical to recognize your power position, and often, a person will realize that they don't have one.

Among the most bizarre decisions I have witnessed are those caused by not taking time to analyze and determine an accurate estimate of one's own power position within the immediate situation.

As you will see below, a narcissist is one who is aware only of their personal reality. They cannot see the reality of others, especially those who may be able to exercise power.

The following are examples of not knowing one's power position:

Teacher/Student

How many times has a student who is dissatisfied with a grade they received on a test decided, in a fit of temper, to go up and give the teacher a piece of their mind? They verbally attack, insult, and abuse the teacher in retaliation for receiving a low grade. If the student needs good or high grades, this is not behavior that will help. The student vents his spleen and feels good for a moment because they really told the teacher off, but in time, reality will set in, and they will have to pay for their actions.

A more effective approach would be to seek a conference with the teacher and respectfully ask what is needed to do better, then to sincerely endeavor to do better and let the teacher see your effort in the work you subsequently turn in.

The first approach is narcissistic, and the second is humble. The narcissistic student sees their own reality, not the teacher's.

The humble student attempts to alter the teacher's vision of reality in favor of the student. The humble student recognizes that it is the teacher who has power in this situation. They adopt a strategy that accepts this fact and try to convince the teacher to view their efforts favorably.

The narcissist attacks with no power and thereby encourages the teacher to respond to the attack at report card time with a low or failing grade. The narcissist has no vision of, or respect for, the teacher's power over their grade.

Typically, in these situations, one person has power, and the other has none. I have witnessed similar altercations between a traffic police officer and the driver receiving the traffic citation, the defendant in criminal court mouthing off to the judge, and countless other situations where powerless people give in to their temper and live to regret it.

These are obvious situations, but others are not. That is why it is always important to consider the possibilities, and if you don't know, beware.

First, consider your power position and your lack of information. Then pick and choose your words and actions carefully, and as a matter of habit and good manners, always be diplomatic. If you are the one with real power, you will be able to run over them if need be, but consider the following.

You never know who you may be dealing with. The young man or woman you encounter may be the child of the chief of police, or a member of an extremely wealthy family, or part of an organized crime family with trained killers at their disposal. Always be diplomatic and use good manners because often you cannot recognize that strangers may have powers of which you are unaware that can destroy your life.

Good manners are the opposite of narcissism. It means that you are considerate of the feelings, position, and reality of others, and you put them ahead of your own position. People with good manners tend to be welcomed anywhere and get along with other people. A famous Mexican saying states that peace is found in respect for the rights of others. (El respecto ajeno es la paz.) A good and effective leader should cultivate good manners and respect for the rights and sensitivities of others as a matter of habit and a hallmark of one's demeanor and performance.

No matter whom you are with or where you are, it is always important, especially for a leader, to know your power position. Someday, you will have one and will need to pick your battles very carefully. Until then, you will have to acknowledge to yourself and accept that, like most people, you really don't have one.

CHAPTER 6
Loss of Perspective

How is it that a leader can have their perspective become compromised and inaccurate?

There are at least three ways, possibly more, that I have observed that can cause a leader to lose perspective:

1. Dealing with a crisis
2. Extreme narcissism
3. The heat of battle

1. Dealing with a Crisis

Psychological Pressure Interplay of Crisis and Perspective

A crisis is defined as a problem without an immediate solution. This leads to a psychological phenomenon like biological inbreeding, in that with each generation, or iteration in one's mind, the affected areas, such as a nose, grows bigger. Every generation, the offspring's nose grows bigger until the nose is the only thing the eventual offspring can see.

Every time a person encounters the problem and realizes that it has no immediate solution, it lingers for a moment, and then the mind wanders to something else. Soon, however, the mind reencounters the problem, and again there is no solution. Thereafter, each time the mind encounters the problem, it becomes bigger and bigger in one's conscious thinking and begins to occupy an unreasonable amount of one's consciousness. It does so without one's recognition.

In one's mind, the problem becomes much bigger than it really is because the person spends so much time thinking about it. This crisis causes a person to lose their perspective. They soon feel endangered, under great pressure, and begin to believe that there may be no way out. The fear that this may be the situation leads to panic in the spirit or a paralysis from fear and an inability to act coherently.

The degree to which a person is affected depends on their previous experiences in dealing with crises. People with a great deal of experience have seen it before and are better able to put the situation in proper perspective.

Many, however, develop what we refer to as pressure blindness, which is generally accompanied by fear and desperation. Pressure and stress-induced blind fear is a terribly debilitating disease. The problem will have grown to gigantic proportions in a person's mind. All they can see is the giant problem in front of them, and they are desperate for an escape. They exist with a sense of the quiet panic of impending doom.

The problem lies with one's lack of an accurate perspective.

Perspective is the ability to see the whole picture; it is the key to a solution. If a person is in Sequoia National Park and looking at a giant redwood with a tree trunk that has a thirty-foot diameter, all that a person can see is this tree. The person can see no way through the forest because all they see is a tree directly in front. This person has no perspective.

If, however, this person is in an airplane flying high above, this person can see several ways through the forest, because the whole picture is visible below. The person now has a better perspective.

When a person is afflicted with pressure-induced blind fear, it is critical that this person regain perspective so that they can regain coherent behavior. To do this, the person needs to heal. It is a real disease, and one's body must heal itself. Generally, it is a good idea to get as far away as possible from the pressure-inducing situation so that one can recharge their batteries and think as little as possible about the crisis. One must put it out of their mind for a while so that the body can heal and put the problem in a proper perspective.

What happens, however, when one's fear is justified because there is real, not just perceived, danger in their situation? When the danger is real, it is even more important to maintain perspective so that decisions are based on positive, logical reasoning and not negative, irrational emotion.

This is best achieved by the perspective gained by experience. There is an old joke that says that good judgment is very important. How does one attain good judgment? Good judgment comes from experience. What causes one to gain experience? Bad judgment. Experienced people have the perspective of having seen it before and generally have the perspective that enables them to act rationally in dangerous situations.

There is another way, however, for a really dangerous situation or when one has no experience in dealing with horrifying situations.

It has to do with acceptance of the situation. Studies have determined that when a person knows that they are going to die, they go through several psychological stages. The first is anger that this situation has occurred to them. The second stage is denial. They try to deny that this is really happening to them. The third is bargaining, an attempt to negotiate a way out. The final stage is acceptance. Calmness comes with acceptance of the inevitable, and rational perspective returns.

An old fighter pilot once said that when he found himself in a difficult situation, he would look ahead to the worst thing that could happen. He would then assume that the worst had happened, and he would deal with it psychologically. Once he had accepted it, the fear was gone. He had accepted the worst; anything else would be a plus. He could now fly with reckless abandon. He could now win. His rational perspective had returned. He was not paralyzed with fear.

When one finds themselves under pressure, it is important that they recognize the danger to their perspective and do things necessary to maintain a healthy perspective.

Many people look to support from friends and relatives to regain and retain their perspective. There is security in knowing that they are not alone and have help. This is comforting. This support can be very effective and, in many cases, can prevent pressure blindness and debilitating fear.

When a person has regained their perspective, it is possible to engage in rational problem-solving. One may look at the crisis and use problem-solving procedures to find a solution to the problem.

2. Extreme Narcissism

The ancient myth of Narcissus tells the story of a beautiful young boy who fell in love with himself because of his personally perceived beauty. His self-love turned into self-adoration. He would choose to indulge is personal self-love (narcissism) by constantly going to a dark pond, where he would kneel on a white rock, lean over, and admire his reflection in the water. The more he did this, the more he wanted to spend time admiring his reflection.

In time, his personal reality that existed only in his head was the only reality that he could see. He could not see the reality of others or of the world around him, especially if it did not agree with his personal reality.

This caused him to lose his perspective concerning the real world around him, which was quite different from the fantasy world in his mind.

One day, totally unconcerned with the real world and totally consumed with the fantasy world in his head, he leaned over to get a better view of himself and lost balance. He fell into the water and drowned.

He had lost his perspective, and it caused his demise. An open, clear, and unobstructed perspective that would have made possible an accurate analysis of his situation and upon which he could have based his actions had become impossible for him. And it killed him.

Moderate Narcissism

Moderate narcissism is healthy. It is important that we like ourselves and feel good about who and what we are. We first must love ourselves before we can feel worthy to be loved by others. It is when narcissism leads to extreme levels that it becomes a sickness causing dysfunctional behavior.

Liquor Analogy

Contemporary medical wisdom holds that a little bit of alcohol is healthy and helps a person relax. Moderation, however, is defined as no more than one or two shots (ounces) two or three times a week. More than this begins the trip into habit, then dependence, leading to addiction and alcoholism. Along the line, a clear perspective is lost, and judgment becomes impaired.

This is like an individual's travel into narcissism, which can lead to extremes and have similar tragic results. Again, perspective and judgment become progressively more impaired. In extreme situations, when one meets such a narcissistic person, it is like meeting a sober person with the perspective and judgment of a drunk. A drunk loses their inhibitions, and their own reality is the only thing that matters to them. They talk incessantly and repeat the same personal concerns repeatedly, with little concern for or recognition of the reality of others. Inebriation appears to be a one-way fast track into narcissism.

This insight led to the realization that narcissism is an underlying cause for engaging in the historic seven deadly sins of envy, greed, pride, lust, gluttony, wrathful vengeance, and slothful laziness. These are known as the cardinal sins, and they all find their origins in narcissism.

The key symptom is the inability to see or accept the reality of others, especially when it conflicts with one's own desires and goals. The narcissist can't see or accept that other people have their own reality and it is different from that of the narcissist.

How does one deal with narcissism?

Just as repeated confrontations with a crisis make the crisis grow so big in the mind that it is the only thing that exists, narcissism that is not checked will also continue to grow. The narcissist will become so engaged in their own reality that their perspective will falter, and they can, like Narcissus, fall into the abyss and perish.

With alcoholism, only the alcoholic can deal directly with their illness; similarly, only the narcissist can cure themselves. Only when there is a genuine desire for the sickness to change can intervention assist. Until then, any attempt at intervention will be viewed as an attack, calling forth an avalanche of defenses and retaliation against the intervenor.

Extreme Narcissism Destroys Perspective

The power of narcissism is such that it entwines itself within the primordial instinct for survival. It calls upon the survival instinct to protect it as it masquerades as the actual person. The narcissist sees criticism of their narcissism as an attack and sets up personal defenses accordingly. Once infected, it takes extreme measures to keep narcissism under control.

I have noticed that many opinionated persons who know they are always right seem to use a filter of personal biases supported by the narcissistic assumption that they already know the true answers and everyone else's opinion is obviously wrong. They really believe it.

What is needed is for the narcissist to recognize on their own that they have a problem. Perhaps a few encounters with objective reality, exposing the narcissist to real pain that a lack of perspective can bring about, may lead to such a realization.

Then it is necessary for the narcissist to regain perspective, heal, and seek to see the reality of others. I knew a friend who would fight narcissism by telling himself over and over, "I am third." *God is first, other people are second, and I am always third.* Once at this point, third-party intervention by a professional may be fruitful.

3. The Heat of Battle

Before going into battle, it is vital that the goals of the engagement be clarified, defined, and communicated to all parties. During the heat of battle, it is easy to get lost, disoriented, and confused as to your immediate objective. Perspective is lost faster here than anywhere else. Your goals serve the same purpose as a goal post in a football game. The objective is clearly visible from all parts of the playing field. If you get disoriented, and it happens often, just look up, and you can ascertain where you are. You regain your perspective.

When you are buried in the confusion and disoriented in the heat of battle, you look for the goal post, or you review your goals and reexamine what is really needed to attain them. Fighting for fighting's sake does not further your objective unless it also brings you closer to your goals. Write your goals down at the beginning and review them often.

CHAPTER 7
A Leader's Perspective and Character

A leader is responsible for others. A leader's ability to effectively solve problems depends on having an open and clear perspective that makes possible accurate analysis, upon which they can base decisions and know when it is necessary to act.

A crisis is a problem without an immediate solution. They come up often. Both subordinates and enemies feed a leader's narcissism and confuse their perspective. Once the battle begins, there is no time for detached analysis. These factors will tear at a leader's perspective.

One key factor in being able to maintain one's perspective is experience.

Every time you go through this kind of pressure, you get better at it. The unknown is terrifying, and experience tends to give you an expectation of what is to be expected. Experience means you are no longer facing the unknown. You have replaced it with an expectation. Curiosity as to the form it will take replaces the terror of not knowing.

A second key factor is a leader's character.

What Is Character?

Character is often defined as who you are in the dark when no one can observe your behavior. One military organization defines character in terms of three values: honor, courage, and commitment.

While definitions differ, I use these abstract concepts to define character as follows: Honor requires one must never lie, cheat, or steal and must exhibit personal integrity, take responsibility for one's actions, and not blame others for one's failures and misfortunes. Courage is the moral and mental discipline to overcome fear and do what is right despite adverse consequences. Commitment is a combination of selfless determination and a relentless dedication to excellence. We, as honorable, courageous, and committed persons, never give up, never give in, and never willingly accept second best. Excellence is always the goal. Commitment never dies. These core values are the foundation that define a good citizen's moral character.

As important as these values are to the development of a strong moral character, there is a deeper level of values that must be the foundation upon which these will stand. These deeper values concern respect for the dignity of humankind and are summed up in one commandment and a familiar quote. The first is from Thomas Jefferson in the American Declaration of Independence, "We hold these truths to be self-evident, that all men are created equal and are endowed by their Creator with certain unalienable rights, that among these are Life, Liberty, and the Pursuit of Happiness." But even more fundamental is the instruction of Jesus Christ, "Blessed are the merciful for they shall obtain mercy" (Matthew 5:7), and his instruction as the great commandment:

> Then one of them, which was a lawyer, asked him a question, tempting him, and saying, Master, which is the great commandment in the law? Jesus said unto him, Thou shalt love the Lord thy God with all thy heart, and with all thy soul, and with all thy mind. This is the first and great commandment. And the second is like unto it, Thou shalt love thy neighbour as thyself. On these two commandments hang all the law and the prophets. (Matthew 22:35–40 KJV)

One important area where I have seen this is ignored is in the care of some children. Children are precious, and they are our future, but they have special needs. I have observed many damaged adults who were traumatized by insensitive adults when they were children. I remember a conversation about the difference between a pediatric dentist and general dentistry. The former is trained not to let the dental experience be a trauma to the child, and special care must be taken while administering anesthesia. Others untrained in this discipline have been so insensitive that children have died in dental chairs. I remember the child television host Mr. Rogers going on a news program and pleading with the reporters at the time of a national tragedy to be heedful of the sensitivities of young children, as to what they were saying and how they were saying it, because it could be harmful to a young child. Children need to be sheltered. They need to feel secure, loved, and protected. Those who are can be a true joy, and those who are not can be severely damaged.

What is the relevance of good character? Why is it important?

Character provides a moral compass when life gets complicated and one must confront difficult decisions involving unpleasant, ambiguous tradeoffs where there are no good options.

The Complicated Tyranny of Life's Tradeoffs

Ideas and experiences that seem simple can quickly become very complicated for one engaging in leadership.

Courage is an example. Courage is not the opposite of cowardice. The opposite of cowardice is foolhardiness. The ancient Greeks came up with the concept of courage being the golden mean between cowardice and foolhardiness. It means that true courage is relative and can differ depending on the circumstances. It is a balance between cowardice and foolhardiness. The moral compass can help one find a proper balance.

The Political Complications of Human Affairs

The real value of character is found when the leader must make political decisions. Any time you have two or more persons together and decisions must be made concerning them and between them, you are in the realm of politics. It can be a treacherous arena, presenting seemingly unlimited and costly tradeoffs, where any decision can entail unpleasant consequences.

Niccolò Machiavelli, in his famous renaissance book *The Prince*, discusses the political qualities that were essential for an effective prince, a political leader in the Italian city-states of the time. Many in the church condemned him because they believed he advocated that a good end justified an improper means to achieve that good end. The church contended that this was a moral error because it would justify any evil if the goal was a good thing. The ends, the church said, does not justify the means.

Fifty years ago, when I was in politics, I read the analysis of a contemporary philosopher activist on this very question. He contended that the church's analysis and the structure of the question was wrong. It really came down to which ends and which means on a case-by-case basis, depending on a lot more facts. A blanket statement made assumptions that would not always apply to variations in the facts.

An example used to make this point was the story of two different political leaders of two city-states of the time. One was James the Just who was a saintly man, and the other was Cesare Borgia, who was not. When a powerful enemy came to conquer and pillage the city ruled by James the Just, his advisors came to him with a plan that required him to lie and engage in deception. He refused because lying was wrong and against his morals. As a result, the city fell, and its citizens were killed or sold into slavery. When Cesare Borgia found himself in a similar situation, he did not hesitate to engage in cowardly lies. The deception worked, and his city survived the attack. Because of his deception, they won the battle. The point Machiavelli would make is that James the Just was a very good man but a very bad prince. Borgia was a bad man but a very good prince. His citizens survived.

Like courage, you have the princely fool, James the Just at one end, and you have the evil genius, Cesare Borgia, at the other end. They were both presented with similar tradeoffs and handled them differently.

What happens when a good man who is neither a fool nor evil is put into a similar situation? Let us look at three historical examples.

The day before D-Day in World War II, the supreme Allied commander, General Eisenhower, met with soldiers of the 101st Airborne Division to encourage them on their role in the coming invasion. They were mainly eighteen- and nineteen-year-old boys and were dressed in combat gear to go straight to their assault planes after the meeting. When they left, Eisenhower went into his study, sat down, and began to shake uncontrollably. His female aide asked what the problem was. He said that he had just sent those young boys into battle but could not tell them that the planners of the battle had projected that by the end of the first day, eight out of every ten would be dead. The tradeoff was a chance to defeat Hitler's Nazi army or the lives of those boys. He had to find the higher morality, and he had to decide. The decision had a profound effect on him.

I am also reminded of the many Christians who risked their lives and sacrificed their fortunes to save the lives of innocent Jews in Nazi Germany.

But what about the price paid to rescue the slaves caught in the worst of all economic traps, American slavery?

The final and most difficult example of character in action is the entire administration of the Lincoln White House during the American Civil War. Initially, Lincoln had incompetent generals and was responsible for allowing them to send thousands of young boys to their death, without any progress being made in pursuit of the war. When he gave the Gettysburg Address, a Chicago newspaper called it silly, flat, dishwatery utterances from a man who did not look like a president. Lincoln performed miracles of administration and leadership and was rewarded with ridicule and eventual assassination. Yet he destroyed slavery and saved the Union. He had to deal with terrible tradeoffs and make hard decisions almost every day.

In each of these cases, character enabled these leaders to have a moral compass to help them maintain a proper perspective and make hard but valid decisions.

CHAPTER 8
On Revolution

Most revolutions are lost just after they have been won. It is more efficient and effective to skip the revolution, recognize your power position, and think of an effective strategy to develop power now within the given constraints. Test your tactics and strategy, learn from defeats, and perfect it through trial and error. As you are successful, your influence and power will grow, allowing the achievement of desired goals.

The turmoil and dislocations resulting from World War II led to many revolutions in its aftermath. The Communist Chinese completed their conquest of China in 1949, Russia grabbed large blocks in Eastern Europe, Central and South America constantly erupted and changed regimes, and in the United States, minorities could not avoid the impulse toward equality. In the 1950s, 1960s, and 1970s, the United States had emerged from World War II as a superpower and was locked in a Cold War with the Soviet Union over whether Russia, using Communist ideology, or the United States, using capitalist and democratic ideologies, would be the surviving superpower.

The Mexican Revolution of 1910 was the backdrop for most Mexican Americans. It was only two generations in the past, and many had heard stories from parents and grandparents about it. American school books did not teach the subject, but Mexican American kids heard about it from oral traditions within their families. As a child in the 1950s, I can still hear my grandfather giving the yell in Spanish, the Grito, "Viva La Revolucion." He had been a rebel and a combatant and told me many stories about it.

In the early 1970s, I was hired as a part-time assistant professor and would soon become chairman of the Department of La Raza Studies at a state university. Many of my students fancied themselves revolutionaries and discussed the seminal work *Anatomy of a Revolution*. It was at that time that I developed the thoughts I am about to discuss.

Most revolutions, I have found, are lost or stolen right after they are won. A revolution creates a power vacuum. The previous source of stability, government, is swept away, and most of the economy is a casualty of war. People need what government and the economy supply, social stability, and basic goods and services, including food, water, and shelter.

In preparing for and fighting the revolution, the new leaders developed effective skills to tear down the previous regime, but generally they never learned how to build. It is easier to tear down that it is to build. Building takes longer, requires capital, and requires a different set of skills that they were never able to take the time to acquire.

Generally, a talented dictator will step into the vacuum and manipulate their way into power. The French Revolution ended with the ascension of Napoleon, who led France to great glory and to total collapse and eventually to Napoleon III, who used the French Foreign Legion and other French forces to invade Mexico to support the Hapsburg Maximillian, the usurper of Mexican sovereignty. The Russian Revolution allowed Stalin to arise. The Chinese Revolution led to Mao Tse Tung's excesses that murdered millions. What makes a great revolutionary is generally not what the people need after the revolution, but the politics are such that a dictator sees the obvious opportunity and cannot resist taking control and evolving into the next oppressor.

Often, I have posed the question, What if we skip the revolution and start building now despite the unfairness we constantly encounter and the often-widespread feelings of oppression? A leader is one who takes the initiative to solve a problem and will start building the new society that is the goal of the revolution. It is easier to build now than it will be in the wasteland that follows a revolution.

Build so that you make the rest of the world irrelevant. Put yourself in a position where you can be self-sufficient and last indefinitely, regardless of whether or not you have available funds. This can be achieved through the concepts of the independent estate, which will be detailed in a future treatise. To summarize it at this point, it entails using new, inexpensive technologies to build a home, an estate that supplies the necessities of life, shelter, electricity, water, waste disposal, permaculture hothouses for growing food, communications, transportation, and so on. It results in an estate that is mortgage-free and independent. What money you do get, save it to grow a capital fund. Capital is defined as wealth used for the creation of more wealth. You will need capital to test new ventures, new technology, and new protocols. Save and use your money for that. Do not consume it on your own appetites.

A Skilled Leader

A critical skill a leader must acquire while building is to ignore naysayers who are very ready to criticize and ridicule early, awkward attempts to build from scratch. Generally, their comments come in one of the following forms: "It will never work," "We were better off before," and "I or others could do a much better job." A leader who is trying to learn how to build must ignore these inevitable comments and the gibberish that accompanies them. Critical naysayers come with the territory. Once you have succeeded in building something new and proving them wrong, the criticism will just escalate. It is a fixture within the territory of leadership. It must be listened to for content initially to see if there is a valid criticism that you can learn from, but once you see that it is normal useless griping, it is to be ignored.

Once in a leadership position, determine what you want to build. That becomes the problem that needs to be solved. Define the problem in detail. Then go to your problem-solving outline included in these materials, and that is how the process begins. Don't be afraid to use trial-and-error experiments to learn as much as possible. This is how most human knowledge was acquired. But once you start, practice constantly and get good at it and get good at building. There will always be a need for the best. Be the best.

When you build well, you create wealth for yourself and your community. When you have wealth, you can again use problem-solving protocols to find ways to become a powerful force in society and use it to achieve equality and justice, making the revolution unnecessary. This is a faster, less painful, positive method of making the oppressors irrelevant and outperforming the purveyors of revolution.

CHAPTER 9
An Educator's Unusual Investment

A Promise That Turned into the Gift of a Lifetime

The True Story of a Young Mexican American Who Became a Leader and Learned How to Fight Powerful Forces to Protect His Family

This is a true story. It happens to be my story, but I know that I am not alone in telling this story. There are many others who will relate to the situations described in this story, but what is remarkable is that there existed an educator who was willing to make a most unusual investment that changed my life—and maybe the world before I am finished.

I know that an adolescent trying to find their way in a new and competitive environment can feel oppressed and inadequate and experience the normal, but very real, fear of the unknown. Yet these young people know that they will soon be expected to meet high expectations and are anxious about meeting challenges that are unfamiliar and that they don't understand.

For a successful outcome to be possible, what is necessary must come from opposite directions. The adolescent must overcome fear with the courage to dare, the willingness to try, and the attitude to accept instruction. The educators must provide the resources that will arouse the curiosity of the young person and challenge them to learn, to discover the relevance and meaning of the materials they are exposed to, and to gain experience leading to proficiency in communicating their thoughts and ideas. The two sides represent mutual resources that need to exploit each other's capabilities.

Many adolescents have self-doubts and question whether or not they have the intellectual and physical ability to be up to the task. When a young African American expressed this fear to James Baldwin, the noted author included a section in his book *The Fire Next Time* where he advised the young man not to worry. He said, "You come from hearty peasant stock" that has endured and will endure despite having to survive unthinkable mistreatment and adverse conditions for generations. But they are still strong and capable today. You, who are alive today, are the descendants of the fit. In a world defined by survival of the fittest, today you are among the fittest. Your competition does not have this advantage.

This is a trait oppressed peoples have in common. Never was it better demonstrated than when Cesar Chavez pitted three hundred poor farm-worker families in open economic combat against the wealthiest and most powerful agricultural interest in California and probably the world. Cesar Chavez led the Grape Boycott Labor Dispute. It represents the only time in history that the poorest of poor went up against the richest of the rich in protracted economic warfare and, after years of struggle, won. The representatives of the rich and proud admitted that the boycott literally brought them to their knees. Such is the power of hearty peasant stock when it has the right leadership, direction, and focus.

How high should a young man strive so as not to be ridiculous and appear foolish? Napoleon Hill, who wrote *Think and Grow Rich,* stated that whatever the mind can conceive and believe, it can accomplish. It is best not to let little minds limit you because they are incapable of comprehending your vision. A Mr. Washington, who was the editor of the *Los Angeles Sentinel* newspaper, continually gave the following advice to young people when they asked for direction on what to do with their lives. He said, "Don't look for what is easy and where the most opportunity is projected to be, but rather find something you like and enjoy, then become the best there is at it." No matter the extent and depth of the competition, there is always room for the best. When President Jimmy Carter was asked by Admiral Hymen Rickover, known as the father of the nuclear submarine program, how well he did at the Naval Academy, Carter responded, "Very well. I was in the upper levels of my class." To which the admiral responded, "Why not the best?" From then on, he always aspired to be the best and eventually was elected president of the United States of America.

So, what was the educator's unusual investment and why was it the gift of a lifetime?

I was born of poor minority parents at the height of World War II when the outcome was still very much in doubt and any reasonable evaluation of my prospects were less than propitious. My immediate family was dysfunctional and eventually broke apart.

I was told, however, by both of my grandmothers, one in English and one in Spanish, that I was very intelligent and I was going to be somebody important. They admonished me to remember that my family was poor and constantly in need of various forms of protection—financial, legal, and, in many cases, physical. I lived in two bad neighborhoods, La Colonia area of Watts and the Hazard Gang Area of East Los Angeles. They told me that if I did not protect them, who would? I was told to never forget my heritage and those who depend on me. A priest told me that to whom much is given, much will be expected. Although I knew that I had gifts from the Almighty, in my view, it seemed that not much of the world agreed.

I grew up feeling that it was my mother, my sister, and I against the world. Strangely, because of my mother, working only with a high school education but with an ability to generate a better than average income through real estate loan commissions, the world did not always seem to win. This set me apart from most of my East Los Angeles neighborhood friends. My mother built a foundation that allowed me to grow and develop. She would take the family on road trip vacations to visit family in Mexico every summer. She moved the family into the suburbs.

Because many of my friends in East Los Angeles had been killed in gang violence, I attempted to make new American friends because it was dangerous to be with Mexicans. These Americans rejected me as different and unacceptable, and soon I again found Mexican friends with whom I could relate. Within two weeks, my newfound Mexican friend "Quinky" was mortally shot in the chest in the parking lot of a neighborhood dance while I watched and thought, *There but for the grace of God go I.*

I decided to walk home in the dark alone for several miles. I was afraid that whoever shot Quinky might be looking to eliminate witnesses. I was fourteen years old at the time and thought that my time to face death and eternity would soon be confronted. I became a loner without friends. They were too dangerous. I started to ask myself questions like "Who am I and what am I here for?" I turned to religion but only seemed to meet fanatics who were not relevant to my quest, but I did find some answers by reading various passages in the Bible. Being a Catholic, I went to confession and got into the state of grace so that I could face death well, with dignity and courage, when the time came.

Then something unexpected began to occur. The more I read, the bigger my world seemed, and I had less and less in common with my previous associates. I was confronted by gang members once on the way home from school because I was carrying a book. To them, that meant I was turning *gabacho* (turning white) and was now a traitor to their identity. I had to fight my way home and from then on snuck home using different routes.

But my world was growing, and I now wanted to know where my family and I came from. What was our history? How did things get the way they were? How did things work and why? I was growing up and needed to be oriented, but how? The church's answers were too limiting and somehow did not meet the promise of the stories in the Bible. The church was all about rules, accounting to have the answers on numbers in the confessional, and being controlled by guilt. The Catholic Church, as I experienced it, was a totalitarian organization where European Spanish priests lorded over the Indian peasants, or the Irish hierarchy exercised paternal domination in God's name. Something was not quite right, but I couldn't put my hand on it. I could see and sense a rebellion as inevitable somewhere down the line. In time, I would notice that we all put money into the collection box, but when it came to the church purchasing goods and services, I never saw any contracts coming our way. I saw a lot going to Irish contractors. There was also a hint toward pedophilia, but I—as did many others, I am sure—dismissed it as absurd.

We are talking about 1958–1960. In or about 1957, the country was rocked by the Soviets launching the first man-made satellite into space, Sputnik. I remember seeing it cross the sky one night. We were in the heights of the Cold War, and it shocked the nation. Soul searching began. *Are the Communists better than us?* Soviet leader Khrushchev constantly boasted that he would bury the United States. We were adversaries in a deadly competition that could destroy the world, and the Soviets seemed to have the advantage in science, technology, and in the competition in the underdeveloped world, especially with their Wars of National Liberation, whereby they would use military means to spread Communism. The biggest were Korea and later Vietnam. The fear that we were losing was real. Eisenhower was a proven leader, but who would replace him? It would not matter if the rest of the nation was not prepared or able to do its part. There was damage to the reputation of our educational institutions, which took a great deal of the blame.

Because of Sputnik, the high school district in our suburban area embarked on an honors program designed to produce leaders, with the idea of being able to compete effectively with the challenges presented by the Soviet Communist system. But there were exceptional teachers at work who saw the program in a greater perspective and wanted to truly enrich the educational experience beyond that of simple competition with the Communists. They assumed that a fully educated citizen, skilled in the ability to think critically, was the best way to prepare the defenders of freedom and that fully programmed automatons designed only to meet today's Communist challenge would eventually prove self-defeating. They set out to give us the broadest possible education, training in critical analysis and thinking and demanding high standards of scholarship. Most of those who experienced it thought it was wonderful. We now had tools that empowered us to deal with the future, the unknown challenges that were sure to emerge and that we would have to confront.

I, however, was not ready for this. Because of the dysfunction of my family, when I entered the tenth grade in high school, I was also entering the tenth different school that I had ever attended. My family had never lived in one district for more than a year. Although I had started reading, I had never read a complete book all the way through. Because I had been stricken with typhoid fever on a trip to Mexico before entering the ninth grade, I was hospitalized and quarantined in the contagious disease ward. I was absent fifty-seven days of my first semester of high school and had a grade point average of D-. The district was building a new high school that would open the following year, and I was set to go there. While waiting to matriculate at my tenth different school, GPA at D-, product of a broken home, minority veteran of the East LA gang wars, I contemplated whether I was the material our nation needed to confront the Soviet menace on the academic front.

Somehow, lurking in the back of my mind was confidence that, if given the opportunity, I could perform admirably. My mother and my family had confidence in my intelligence and ability even if no one else did, and that was all I needed to try. Despite the dysfunction, my mother had been a stabilizing force in my life. Like most young Mexican Americans, I felt protected and loved unconditionally, and I had a genuine sense of self-value.

Then lightning began to strike, and fate took a helping hand. While in class one morning, a representative from the principal's office came to my classroom and said I had been ordered by the principal to go to a certain classroom. There were people there who needed to talk me. Everyone ordered there, including me, thought that we must be in real trouble. When I arrived at the designated class room, I found about twenty other students there. They were all white and appeared to me to be the elite. A teacher stood up and announced that the district had, in response to Sputnik, embarked upon an honors program to develop leaders to meet the Soviet challenge. The program would have high standards and required exceptional effort. To gain entrance, an applicant would have to submit three recommendation letters, take an aptitude test, submit a formal application, and pass a personal interview examination into their willingness to submit to the rigors that would be encountered. They wanted only the best prepared and most motivated. The program was new, and they did not want to take any chance that anyone selected would not be successful.

The students all looked at one another. Some wondered what that Mexican was doing there. The teacher said that if we were there, it was because one or more teachers who knew us felt that we had what it would take to be successful. I wanted very much to be part of this. I wanted my questions about life answered, and I wanted to be among the elite. Now there would be a chance.

Everything went fine until the interview. The two interviewers had my entire record in front of them and were aware of its shortcomings. They began by politely telling me that next year things might be different in a new school and that I could apply again at that time. I could see that I was being turned down, and it hurt. I had to grit my teeth to keep from crying, but tears rolled down my checks. The interviewers were astonished. They knew me and knew that I was sincerely disappointed. They were embarrassed by the turn of events. I could not talk. They decided that they would not turn me down but would look for a way for me to participate. They told me to wait to hear from them.

I understand that that night there was a terrible clash within the governing board. There were those who wanted only the best and would not take a chance on failures. The other group argued that they should not discount student desire and perseverance. Eventually, a probationary program was agreed to, and I was admitted on condition that my GPA rose to a B for the last quarter of the semester. In the final tally, I understand that seven students were admitted on probation, including me. I earned an A average for the quarter and a B for the semester and gained admittance. Of the seven, I was the only one who successfully gained admittance. The others were not motivated to work as hard as I did. I felt that I was fighting for my life and my family's future.

Once classes started, however, the going was rough. The other students were better trained, very conscientious, and smart. I could not write or spell anywhere near what was required. I felt totally incompetent and knew that I did not belong with these very good students. So many things that they took for granted, I had never heard of. About half were white middle-class kids from the elite families of the area. The other half seem to be composed of nerds and well-behaved working-class overachievers. I stood out like a wart. One of my best teachers, although he died at age forty, had a profound effect on many students but especially on me. I wrote a paper for him that was a page and a half long. He wrote me back a three-page paper in red ink telling me that I was illiterate and unless I learned to write and spell, I would be crucified as I tried to advance. He later told me that although he wanted minorities like me to advance, he did not make a big effort for them because he found that invariably they would get discouraged and quit.

I thought to myself, *I don't quit.* My father, who had played professional football, had indoctrinated me with too much football to give up. Among other things, I was a football player and had made the team even though I had missed fifty-seven days of school. As soon as I learned to walk, I was taught how to block and tackle. However, I was small, and everyone told me that I was too small for football, that I was going to get hurt playing much bigger and stronger athletes. I asked my grandpa, who taught me how make shoestring tackles, if I was too small. His answer was one for the ages. He said, "If your heart is big enough, then you're big enough." That settled it. I was going to play. After missing a lot of time due to illness, I requested and was permitted to challenge for a spot on the team. By the end of my first week, I was playing on the first team. By the end of the next year, I would be captain of the varsity at the new school. Once I am in the battle, I am not about to give up. But I knew how to play football. And it was 80 percent desire, 20 percent skill. But I did not know how to learn to write. I did the best I could, but it was all wrong. I was ready to accept that I might go down fighting, but I would never quit.

Perseverance is a wonderful thing. I learned on the football field to play for a break and be ready to seize it when it comes, and it comes when least expected. Apparently, news of my challenges got around. One of my teachers had been one of my interviewers when tears started flowing down my cheeks. He was also a coach of the smaller Class B football team. He was also a former Marine Corps Drill Instructor. He arranged for both of us to be excused one day from practice. He told me to report to his classroom instead of football practice on a Monday. My varsity coaches confirmed this. I did not have a clue as to what was up. It would turn out to be one of the most important days of my life.

This teacher had decided to invest some of his time with me in an unusual experiment. This teacher may have been new to academic teaching, but he knew a thing or two about developing men. He was a Marine Corps veteran of the Korean War. He had fought at the Chosen Reservoir and had been a drill instructor at Camp Pendleton. He taught school like the DI that he was. One did not contradict him.

He had me come into his classroom. No one else was there. He stood up at the lectern and opened his notes. He had me sit at the desk right in front of him. He then informed me that he was going to attempt to teach me how to write in one lecture.

But first we had to get certain things out of the way. He expected me to be a scholar. But more to the point, he expected me to be the best of scholars. He wasn't interested in going further unless I was prepared to pay any price, bear any burden, and do any and all things necessary to be the best. He did not want to deal with second best; only the best would do. And if I did not have the guts to put in the unreasonable amount of work necessary to be the best, then he did not want to bother with me.

Then he made the promise that changed my life. He said if, however, I was willing to make the effort, whatever the cost, then he said, "I will teach you how." Those words: I will teach you how. I will teach you how to be the best. It might as well have been "I will save your life." "I will make your life meaningful." "I will give you a chance to walk among giants." "I will give you the opportunity to earn the secret knowledge of how and thereby give you the power to be or do anything."

I listened and thanked him. Results did not come immediately. I apologized one day because I knew my paper did not meet his standards, but he said I was making progress. He could see the effort and that it was working because the improvement was obvious. He said to just stick with it, and over time, I would be fine. By the end of the year, I had developed my own writing style and had very few misspelled words. I seemed to have no problem communicating. Writing had become a nonissue.

What I really learned was how to make the effort to effectively teach myself how to do anything. I learned that I could research and report my findings and learn from my scholarly efforts. I was on my way, and the question of how would never again be a barrier.

When other people believe in you and continue to believe in you, you can feel that you have permission to believe in yourself. It doesn't happen all at once, but with perseverance, there is little you can't do. The ability and willingness to persevere, to never give up, is among the best predictors of success that exist.

I went to college on a football scholarship, then to law school. I became an attorney and was appointed a planning commissioner, then the highest-ranking Hispanic official in city government. I was elected the state's at large delegate to the 1976 Democratic National Convention, and I became chairman of the board of a national bank.

Then I left all of that to take on the most important challenge that I could face, and I shall write about that when it is over. Now, however, I am clearly losing, and to a reasonable observer, it would appear obvious that there is no way I can succeed, but I have been in that position before, and the thought of giving up has never entered my mind.

I want the readers of this book to strive to be the best at what they do. This book attempts to fulfill the same promise.

If you are ready to make the effort required, this book
provides the lessons that will teach you how!

CHAPTER 10

Life Lessons from Basic Seal Training

Below is a summary of an inspiring and powerful twenty-minute commencement speech by Naval Admiral William H. McRaven at the university-wide commencement at the University of Texas at Austin on May 17, 2014.

> Start each day with a task completed. Find someone to help you through life. Respect everyone … Life is not fair; you will fail often … Take some risks, step up when the times are toughest, face down bullies, lift the downtrodden and never, ever give up … It matters not your gender, your ethnic or religious background, your orientation, or your social status. Our struggles … are similar … Changing the world can happen anywhere and anyone can do it.

PART II

Lessons for Life as an Effective Person

LESSON 1
Threats and Gambles

I try to never threaten and never gamble. Rather than making a threat to do something, I just do it. If you are serious, a threat just warns the adversary.

I once had a friend who I found was very manipulative. Soon I needed to cut off the relationship. I remember later having a conversation with him where he told me that he had mistakenly judged my being nice for being weak. When he devised ways to threaten me, he found that I had no problem going my own way, despite the potential negative consequences of not submitting to other people's will.

These threats were both social and physical. I learned early to challenge immediately and dare them to follow through. I learned to be prepared for a fight and the consequences of my actions. I found that many people who threaten people who appear to be weak are bullies. Bullies want easy pickings and do not like dealing with people who fight back. They have little inclination to deal with a direct challenge and tend to back down. If they don't back down, then it is important to deter future bullying by making them pay a costly and painful price.

If you have a reputation for gambling, you will find yourself constantly tested and your gambles called. There are times, however, when the situation leaves you little or no alternative, and you must gamble.

I encountered such a situation when I was researching the reasonable, as compared to the necessary, during a wartime situation. The person everyone was depending upon stated that he was making every reasonable effort and doing his best. The general responded, "Your reasonable efforts will kill us all. If you can't get done what is necessary, we must find someone who can. Since there is no one else, *you* must rise to the occasion and find a way to keep us alive."

When desperate and out of options, where any action seems hopeless, I look to history for inspiration. How did other leaders who found themselves confronted with severe adversity succeed anyway?

For me, the last time was when I had run out of money in the middle of a development and construction project. I needed $60,000 a week for ten weeks and did not have it. This was at a time when $60,000 was a lot of money. The situation was grim. The company was facing disaster and failure as a going enterprise.

I found my inspiration by the way the Union officers acquitted themselves at Little Round Top during the Battle of Gettysburg, which was a decisive turning point in the American Civil War. They were out of ammunition, under attack, and about to be overwhelmed. Pondering what to do, the Union commander decided to devise and implement a counterattack. The elements of surprise, audacity, and maneuver would have to perform despite a lack of ammunition. As the other side attacked up the hill, they charged down the hill, surprising, confusing, and routing the enemy, who was not aware that they had no bullets for their weapons.

I changed my tactics. Despite being completely out of money, I assumed the demeanor of a person flush with cash. I started making demands, threatening lawsuits, which would halt the project and be costly to everyone, and refusing to put out any more money until my demands were met. I accomplished everything I needed without spending a cent.

I gave myself a chance to be lucky.

LESSON 2
An Outline of Leadership

The concept of leadership is complicated and subject to interpretations.

Due to the nature of our analysis, we divide the concept of leadership into two areas, substantive leadership and a leader's presentation brand, sometimes referred to as style.

The development of substantive leadership requires the following:

Definition: A Leader is a person who takes the initiative in solving problems faced by persons having a community of interest.

The quality of a leader is determined by how effective they are in mobilizing others in need at taking action that is effective and achieves objectives.

These are the essential qualities of effective substantive leaders. The experience and exercise they receive in engaging in the protocols of problem-solving prepares them to recognize problems and opportunities. But it also makes them knowledgeable, experienced, and prepared concerning the elements and operations that are affected by their problem-solving activities. As result of this activity, when they discuss these issues, they are to be taken seriously because now:

1. They know what they are talking about;
2. They mean what they say; and, of utmost importance,
3. They can make it happen.

A leader who is sufficiently effective at making it happen has learned how to solve and overcome the problems presented by adversity, generally in the form of barriers, obstacles, and adversaries. Adversity tends to include the following:

1. Fear of the unknown;
2. Insufficient resources (especially money and time); and
3. Vocal ridicule and opposition from naysayers, competitors, and adversaries.

To develop and improve the qualities of effective leadership requires that a leader, who is constantly improving and developing their skills, become proficient in the art of recognition and the ability to maintain or regain an accurate perspective in situations that tend to distort reality.

LESSON 3
Presentation Brand

The way you dress and present yourself determines how you will be treated by other people. Your appearance is your presentation to the world and is extremely important to your effectiveness. It is the beginning of your presentation brand.

The development of a leader's presentation brand is determined by their demeanor, appearance, and ability to communicate. This is enhanced by the quality of their team of associates and their use of status symbols.

A tragedy of leadership is when a politician develops an effective brand and patina but has no substance whatsoever and is unable to be effective or accomplish anything of value.

Great leadership requires substantive effectiveness and a charismatic or appealing presentation brand. This is the style to go with the substance. Both are equally important to effectiveness.

Substance is the ability to recognize problems, to recognize opportunities, to develop problem-solving skills, and to maintain an accurate understanding of the situation during difficult moments. Style is to look good and set an example for others while leading. These are what are required of an individual to be an effective leader and are the elements of style and substance. (Materials and concepts on substance were the subject matter covered in chapters 1 through 10.)

LESSON 4
It Is Incredibly Easy to Let Other People Ruin Your Life

It is important to make your own decisions and not let others, even close friends or relatives, think for you.

Sometimes damage is unintentional, but other times it is malicious, intentional, and the most insidious form of betrayal. Because it comes from people you trust and respect, it is extremely difficult to recognize.

A course I once took in critical thinking caused me to become ruthless in checking my facts and evaluating the opinions and advice of others to determine the validity of their opinions and the truthfulness of their representations. On several occasions, when I discovered facts and betrayal that I would never have suspected, this ruthless fact-checking proved to be my salvation.

Be suspicious when others want to make decisions for you.

Strangers

Be especially cautious when strangers confront you with a smile like they are your close friend. Most people who don't know you will give you a polite smile to be nice, or they will just ignore you. But if they go out of their way to come toward you with a smile out front, they are after something. They don't know you, so why are they being so nice and attentive to you? There are reasons for their interest in you. They may have designs that are in their interest but at your expense. A smile from a stranger, in my experience, generally means that a knife in the back is coming quickly. Songwriters Norman Whitfield and Barrett Strong made a valid point in their lyrics to the song "Smiling Faces" when they stated that "a friend is an enemy you can't see." These situations can present difficult judgment calls. Just make sure that while you contemplate, your defenses are up and your escape routes are clear. If they start to close, make a dash for the exit.

Betrayal

I have seen betrayal by people who pretend to be friends but are vicious wolves with incredible guile. Ignore what a person says; judge them by their actions. Do they do things that are in your interest and that have a cost to them? Do they do things that are not in their interest, but they do them anyway to help you? Or is everything in their interest and at your expense, repeatedly? Christ said in his sermon on the mount that "by their fruits you shall know them"(Matthew 7:20 DRA). There are several former friends that I have had to avoid and separate myself from because of the negative effect they have had on my life. Because they were my friends, I expected and assumed that they had my back and would protect me. It took a while to recognize, but I realized it was my responsibility, and not that of my so-called friends, to protect my life and the interests of those who depend on me.

This lesson is about dangers posed by others, especially by unseen enemies. In addition to the above and based on my personal experience, I will also describe situational danger, danger by well-meaning friends and relatives, psychological damage those close to you can inflict, and insidious dangers from unseen, powerful, indiscriminate interests that could care less about the damage they cause.

Situational Awareness

Situational awareness is probably the most relevant and important skill one can develop. When I ran a medical center in San Francisco during the hippy, flower-power invasion of the mid-1960s, I had occasion to meet with the director of the Haight Free Clinic about health concerns being treated at the neighborhood level. The hippies preached free love, giving rather than greed, and did not trust authority or anybody over thirty. Make love not war was their motto. They invaded the Haight Ashbury District of San Francisco. They left themselves vulnerable, and it wasn't long before a criminal element moved in to exploit their vulnerability. Drug dealers, muggers, and rapists had a field day, with little of it being reported. Soon the invasion witnessed the death of twenty hippy young people. My counterpart at the Haight Free Clinic studied the murders and explained the tragedy to me with the following analysis. He said that all the kids that had been murdered were from the Midwest and had no familiarity with the culture of crime and therefore had no concept of situational awareness. They did not recognize that they were in a dangerous situation until it was too late.

I grew up in what amounted to a gang war zone in East Los Angeles. Gang fights, drive-by shootings, mugging, robberies, and violence were commonplace. Living there taught everyone to be aware of their situation and cognizant of the potential for danger. The way to deal with danger was to recognize the possibility and avoid it. Situational awareness means that you are keenly aware of your surroundings and can sense when danger may be developing around you. You move and get out of the situation before it turns dangerous. People without situational awareness do not see the danger and walk right into situations that can kill them. As I said earlier, situational awareness is probably one of the most relevant and important skills one can develop.

The Well-Meaning Relative or Friend

One must also consider the well-meaning but misinformed relative or friend who wants to be helpful. Damage can occur in the most unexpected ways. My maternal grandmother loved me dearly when I was young, but she had been born and raised in Mexico and brought up with a keen work ethic and Christian Catholic values. When I graduated from high school, I enrolled in a four-year private college where I received a football scholarship. As my grandmother understood it, I went to college to play football while my mother was struggling financially, as were we all. My grandmother started a campaign to make me quit college and go to work to help my mother. She said that I owed my mother my help rather than having fun going to college. She put great pressure on my mother for letting me do what I wanted to do. My mother already had too much pressure, and this made it worse. My grandmother had no appreciation for the value of a college education. She did what she thought was best for all of us. She was showing her love for us. She just did not know any better because of her background. This did not change until she found out that my college degree qualified me to attend a great law school and that I was probably going to be an attorney. Just prior to her death and after I entered law school, I became, in her mind, the saint who could do no wrong. These situations do not always end up on a positive note. They can be tragic.

Of all the ways in which other people can hurt, the worst are also the two seldom recognized by an individual. These are the following:

The Damaged Psyche

The first is the psychological damage those close to you can inflict, especially if you trust them and they want to maintain a position of dominance over you. I was once attacked by a smart legal and business interest who wanted to destroy my effectiveness because I was advocating a city policy that could be very costly to them. They put together a brilliant plan to compromise me, creating vulnerability, and then quickly seized upon the vulnerability to permanently cripple me and keep me out of their hair. I had always been told that any lawyer who represents themselves has a fool for a lawyer. I hired a friend to represent me, who immediately embarked upon a campaign to convince me that I was incompetent in this area of the law where he was a specialist. Anything I said or suggested was wrong. I believed him, and as time went on, I began to doubt myself. I lost my self-confidence and believed that he was correct, would always be correct, and that I would always be wrong. His credentials in this area were impeccable, and mine were nonexistent. Later I realized that he had done this on purpose to pressure me to pay him a great deal of money, which I did. The case did not go well for me, and he made me believe that the cards were stacked against us to the point where we had no chance of winning but could only depend on him to use his influence to mitigate my impossible situation. Then a situation came up that forced him off the case to deal with his diagnosis of cancer.

I had to take over the case myself because I had no more money. He had bled me dry. But something funny happened. Things began to go better, despite my loss of confidence and a paralysis of fear. I resolved the situation without him, and he died soon after. The psychological damage to my psyche was great and palpable. I believed a friend who had a financial interest in bringing me down. It took years to regain my swagger. I lost a great deal of valuable time that I am trying to regain now. No one, in a frontal attack, could have damaged and weakened me like this so-called friend did while supposedly trying to help me. And at the time, I could not see it.

The Unseen Force

There are forces that have enormous influence and virtually unlimited funds that are at work improving their circumstances at the public expense in general and at your expense in particular. I can't tell you who they are, but I can share my evidence and reasoning. There are bad drugs on the market that only treat symptoms and do not cure. These are more profitable to the drug companies. When you cure a patient, you lose them. When you only treat a symptom, they remain your patient forever, paying for their medication. Both the drug companies and the oil companies abuse their power and raise prices to unconscionable levels because they know they can get away with it and there is little we can do about it. Competition does not effectively exist in either marketplace.

My strategy for dealing with these forces is to make them irrelevant. I find substitutes in herbal medicine that may work slower but do work. I also have developed technology to make my own fuel. This will be the subject of a future treatise, which is about how to eliminate vulnerabilities and employ technological substitutes for products and commodities currently controlled by monopolies and oligarchies.

LESSON 5

Political and Economic Power in the Twentieth Century

(How Football, Teachers, and Coaches Lied to Me)

Let's start with my view of the twentieth century, where I spent the bulk of my life. The way power, economics, and religion worked for me was that they all lied to me. The biggest, most devastating lies came from my well-meaning high school football coach and some teachers.

My football coach wanted to build character. He taught me to go out on a level playing field, compete physically and mentally, and outperform the other guy. There were officials to enforce fairness, and everyone knew the rules of the game and what was expected. Either you performed or you did not, and there was immediate accountability. "If you can't handle it, we will put in someone who can." I was full of desire, worked very hard, got better, and eventually was named captain of the varsity and Outstanding Senior Athlete. I was awarded a football scholarship to Whittier College. I was, and am still, full of character, integrity, and perseverance.

But they lied about the terrain, the real obstacles, and the ammunition required. When I left college, I found that the world did not provide a level playing field, but everyone tried to maintain a level of leveraged advantage over everyone else. There was no accountability, and nothing was fair. Except for the violence and viciousness, nothing in real life resembled the football field.

Then my coach echoed my teachers in implying that money was evil and not to be effectively sought after. Religion, family, and home were more important. Seeking after money was a sin of greed. A decent wage for honest work was good. A lot of money is bad. And I believed it and did not make financial accumulation one of my goals.

I remember seeing an article in the newspaper about a young high school baseball player who was offered over a million-dollar bonus to sign with the New York Yankees and turned it down because all his life he had wanted to play for the LA Dodgers. He signed with the Dodgers for about $200,000 and never got to the majors. At the time, an *LA Times* sports reporter wrote in a newspaper column that, unfortunately, this kid hadn't learned yet that money is everything.

What became very important to me later was protecting my family and giving my cousins in the greater Mexican American community a fair shot at making something of their lives. It then became clear that money was power, and power was fundamental to doing anything. My teachers and coaches were all about character, responsibility, and hard work. They had long ago given up on having money. They did not seem to recognize its connection to, or the need for, power in society. Their psychological defense was that big money and greed were synonymous, and it was bad and to be avoided. You may not get rich doing what they do, but (the biggest lie of all) you will have a great life if you just stay right here and don't aspire for too high a goal. You can try to be rich, but even if you succeed, you will be miserable with your life. Rich people must do too many mean things to people to get rich and therefore can never be happy with only a lot of money.

So, don't seek to be wealthy. You can vote but stay out of politics because it is dirty and corrupt. Get a job, work hard, buy a home, have a family that is honest and hardworking, and sit back and enjoy your retirement. The law is just and will protect you. People at the top are responsible and will do the right thing for you and your family. Know your place, and you will be fine.

If there are problems with the system, eventually it will come before the ballot, and the public, the people, will settle the matter. Work hard, be good, don't cause trouble, be punctual, be a good employee, and the company will reward you with a good salary reflecting your worth. Use it to buy a house and raise a good family. That is the good life to which all good, responsible people should aspire.

What a crock! They really believed what they preached and thought they were helping me by showing me how to stay on the straight and narrow path to success, which was a house and a pension check. Blessed are the meek for they shall inherit the earth (Matthew 5:5 KJV). (Later I would remember the movie where the Mexican bandit says, "Si senor, but only six feet of it,")

The problem for me and many of the honors program students was that we wanted to create change and make justice real. But we never learned how to make money along the way. We did not realize it at the time, but we were creating a terrible handicap that we would later have to overcome. We believed that being active in civic affairs would lead to government taking appropriate action to right wrongs. Upon graduation and entering the real world, we were quickly informed that money is the mother's milk of politics. You can't do anything without it, and if you don't have money, you have no power.

What my teachers and coaches really taught me was to stay out of trouble and be an ineffective pawn in the game of power, politics, and government. Forget about concepts of self-determination and power over my own destiny. What they really advocated was putting my family's fate in the hands of entities over which I would be powerless to influence. I learned very quickly that in American society, money is power, and words alone are meaningless conversation.

In the real world, money buys votes, buys power, and buys influence, and if you don't have it, you don't count, and you don't matter at all. Thanks, fellows, for letting me think there is justice in the world and that right makes might—but mostly for teaching me not to make accumulating wealth a priority because that is beyond our station and probably our capabilities.

Where Wealth Plays a Role

Before I went out into the world, I had been involved in student politics and was elected student body president of my high school. It was 1960, and I followed the career of John Kennedy. His presidential debates with Richard Nixon made me feel that I could have a career in politics. At the time, I was unaware of the role money played in politics or in life, beyond just being able to pay your bills.

I had noticed that everyone in my high school honors classes had concluded that Stuart Symington, senator from Missouri, was the most qualified Democrat and therefore would be nominated by the Democratic Party. My research showed that the top contenders in 1960 were Symington, Hubert Humphrey, the liberal senator from Minnesota, Lyndon Johnson, the former segregationist senator from Texas, and what looked like a young upstart, John Kennedy, the war hero and journalist son of a wealthy businessman and former ambassador to England, Joseph P. Kennedy.

I remember reading a *Time* magazine article that evaluated the prospects of all the candidates. They also concluded that Symington was the logical choice. The article seemed to sneer that all Kennedy had was youth and money. The key to Kennedy's winning the nomination was defeating Hubert Humphrey in West Virginia, a Protestant state. At the time, Kennedy's Catholic religion was considered his greatest vulnerability. Protestants and Republicans were concerned that his election would put the pope in the White House. The day after the West Virginia primary election, Congressman George Kasem, my first political mentor, had breakfast with a very bitter Senator Humphrey, who complained that the Kennedys had literally bought the election with what seemed like unlimited funds.

Joe Kennedy's estimated $450,000,000 was used to guarantee his son the nomination and the general election. The race with Richard Nixon in the general election was very close and exciting. Illinois proved to be the key. Kennedy had to win there or lose the election. He won by twenty thousand votes, a razor-thin margin. Much later, speculation claimed that the fifty thousand dead Chicagoans that supposedly were voted by the Cook County Democratic machine was the real difference. In classic fashion, it now appears that the Democrats stole the election with a great assist from Joe Kennedy's money.

Later when Al Gore was defeated by George W. Bush, it appears that the Republicans returned the favor with a great assist from a Supreme Court controlled by Republican appointees.

George Kasem lost his congressional race and, with my help, tried to get reelected two years later. He was defeated in the primary election by a candidate supported by Jesse Unruh, the portly thirty-nine-year-old Speaker of the state assembly who had taken control of lobbyist money by demanding all contributions be made to his minions and that he would dole it out to deserving candidates, his candidates. It was the Unruh machine. Jesse Unruh claimed openly that "money was the mother's milk of politics," and he used his power over the state assembly to gain control over the big campaign contributions. These funds paid for mailing campaign letters that cost hundreds of thousands of dollars. The candidate without money was invisible. In the Southern California suburban battleground in which we were engaged, mailings were the deciding factor. Unruh backed his slate with the money he had extorted, and that slate did not include an independent-minded George Kasem. Kasem lost, but his ally, George E. Brown, won in the adjacent district. As a favor to Kasem, Congressman Brown agreed to sponsor me as an intern in Washington, DC, on Capitol Hill in the summer of 1963. Many of Jesse Unruh's tactics are now illegal, and political contributions are regulated by California Fair Political Practices Commission.

Congressman Brown was able to engineer a presidential appointment by President John F. Kennedy for me as a summer intern in the Labor Department as a GS-2, the lowest of the low but not bad for a nineteen-year-old nobody from California.

All I really had going for me was the very practical education I had learned in the primary wars within the Democratic Party fighting Jesse Unruh's machine. The first rule was that there were no rules. Winning the election was all that mattered. Treachery and power politics fueled by cash ruled the day. Even though I was very honest and sincere with the best of intentions, I seemed to have a talent for this political world and took to it like a duck to water. I learned the unwritten rules and began to play them very well.

Times have changed. There was a consensus among my coworkers that the democracy we worked in was flawed because money welded by the rich gave them excessive power. The power of wealthy made our world, we felt, a functioning plutocracy. Today, however, the internet has changed how our democracy is financed. Today, the internet and social media make it possible to communicate with the masses without having to spend hundreds of thousands of dollars on mass mailing campaigns. Furthermore, it is now possible to efficiently finance a message and have a voice that only the rich had in the past. A one-dollar contribution from a million small contributors can amass a million dollars to match a rich person's million-dollar donation. The internet has brought more economic democracy. A united class of small contributors can now match the financial influence of a rich contributor. Both now have standing and the potential to be equally effective politically.

Once in Washington, DC, I found myself among the eastern Ivy League elite. I was a student at Whittier College, Richard Nixon's alma mater, which seemed to make me acceptable. Stanford was the only school on the West Coast to send interns back to Washington, DC. Most of these students were well to do, but all were interested in politics, and I was the one who had practical knowledge and had gotten back there through my political activity. This put me in an exclusive class by myself, and I became totally accepted. I learned about Ivy League values that summer. Being from the East Los Angeles barrio via Watts, I grew very fast. That was the summer that Martin Luther King gave his "I Have a Dream" speech, and I nearly got myself killed by the KKK on a mission to Savannah, Georgia, to aid an imprisoned civil rights worker from UCLA. I originally travelled by Greyhound bus when I went to DC, but I returned to Los Angeles by jet airplane. That is how much I changed that summer. Within three months of my return, John Kennedy was assassinated. I was now an active participant in the real world.

What I learned was that money was important if you wanted to be able to protect your family and have control over your destiny. That realization, however, was not the beginning of a solution but rather an introduction into a whole new set of complexities that will be explored in subsequent lessons for life herein.

LESSON 6

Taking on the Super Big and Powerful

Entities, be they persons, institutions, or countries, can develop technologies, protocols, and methods that make them more powerful than they seem. Many times, these entities with latent power seem like they would be easy to bully, and both the intentional and the inadvertent bully can end up getting a bloody nose when they attempt to abuse these seemingly weak persons.

The Vietnam people repelled and defeated an invasion by Kublai Khan's Mongolian Empire both on land and on sea in the thirteenth century when the Mongolians were the most powerful force on the planet. They were not able to subdue this tiny little country even though they had conquered all the land from China to Eastern Europe. Western European areas just weren't worth their interest, or they would have taken them also.

The all-powerful Mongolians tried to subdue little Vietnam and failed. Nor did China ever conquer Vietnam. In modern times, the iconic Vietnam General Vo Nguyen Giap is famous because he found a way to defeat the Japanese invasion during World War II, then defeat the French colonial empire, then the Americans who were trying to stop Communist expansion, then another Chinese incursion, and finally Pole Pot's Cambodia to stop their killing fields.

How did they defeat the American military, the most sophisticated and powerful in the world? Right-wing politicians blame the American Vietnam War protestors for the defeat, claiming they gave treasonous aid and comfort to the enemy. It gives them comfort to believe this. We were not beaten; it was our traitors who sold us out, they whine. Sounds like Hitler explaining Germany's loss in World War I. The truth lies elsewhere.

Statements from Vietnam after the war indicated that they felt that the leaders in the United States did not know very much about them. They said that Thomas Jefferson would have had a better idea. He wrote their ideals in the American Declaration of Independence. They value their freedom and sovereignty. They have protected it at all costs for centuries against seemingly more powerful adversaries. They literally would pay any price to protect it. They have always had to fight and have gotten very good at it. They defeated the Japanese and the French. The Americans are just a stronger version of the same. In the end, they reasoned, the result will be the same.

I remember reading an article concerning an interview with two American generals in Vietnam at the beginning of our build-up around 1965. They were asked if they were going to consult the French generals to gain a better understanding of what they would be facing and get their ideas on how to win. These generals were insulted by the question. Their arrogance was beyond belief. They said no, they had nothing to learn from the French. The French had been defeated. They said that they would have to learn from their own mistakes in the field. The truth is that they could not conceive of any possible way they could lose. There was a time when the French generals also felt that way. Is it really a surprise that a people, fighting on their home soil, who had defeated the Mongolians at the height of their power, would not be afraid to fight the French or the Americans? That they would be willing to pay whatever the price would be for the survival of their homeland. This, and the implications flowing from it, is what the American leaders did not understand.

General Giap, in interviews after the war, stated that the idea to defeat the Americans came from reading T.E. Lawrence's book, *Seven Pillars of Wisdom*. While gravely ill with a fever, Lawrence of Arabia had a revelation about how the lowly Saudis could force the Ottoman Turks out of Saudi Arabia during World War I. He reasoned that control of Arabia was not vital to the survival of the Turkish Empire. Therefore, he reasoned, if you make it costly enough long enough, they will leave. That is exactly what happened.

General Giap postulated, "Is Viet Nam vital to the survival of the United States? The answer is NO. Therefore, if you make it costly enough long enough, they will leave." After losing more than fifty thousand Americans in Vietnam, the 1968 TET Offensive proved that any victory would require far more lives than the American people would accept. The antiwar movement was a response to revelations that the Gulf of Tonkin Congressional Resolution giving the president the power to wage the war was procured by fraud. The incidents attributed by the military to North Vietnam never occurred. The Pentagon Papers published by the *Washington Post* newspaper showed that the military had been lying to the American people concerning prospects in Vietnam. The actions of the protestors were a legitimate exercise of free speech in response to the lies they had been told.

Because the United States, as a powerful military power, could not impose its will arbitrarily on the small country of Vietnam, the right-wing politicians stated that we had lost the war in Vietnam because of the left-wing antiwar protestors. The prevailing sentiment is that we lost in Vietnam.

I see it differently. We did not go into Vietnam to prove that we could beat up a little nation. The rationale for engaging in Vietnam was to halt the expansion of Communism by military aggression. It was believed that Vietnam would be a domino causing the other nations of Southeast Asia to fall like dominos to the Communist through military aggression. This was called the domino theory.

If one holds to a racist concept that if a superior force of white men, and minorities lead by whites, could not impose their will on a smaller bunch of yellow men, then they have lost, then maybe one could argue that we lost.

But forget about racial prejudice and consider the following. Our strategic mission in Vietnam was halting Communist military aggression. We paid a high price, fifty-five thousand American lives lost. For the people of Vietnam, it was victory at any price; their survival as an independent sovereign state was at stake. To remain free of foreign control, stay in control of their own land and society, and to be protected from American domination cost them two million lives—two million from that little country.

Because of the war, the new reality was that it was now far too costly for the Communists to engage in military aggression. The price of defending against the Americans was far too high to continue. The strategic mission of the United States was accomplished. The dominos did not fall. A high price was paid, but it was mission accomplished concerning the strategic objective. In a larger sense, both sides paid an unacceptable price; there were no winners.

A Nonmilitary Example

In the twentieth century, impoverished members of Cesar Chavez's United Farm Workers Union declared a grape boycott against California's largest, richest, and most powerful industry, agribusiness, to win the right to unionize farm workers in California. It was literally the poorest of the poor against the richest of the rich in open economic warfare. To match the power of money, Chavez dispatched hundreds of families and individuals to organize the boycott in the urban centers, depending mostly upon community support to sustain these families. These families were used to living an impoverished lifestyle, and this mission was just more of the same. Their poverty and determination spoke volumes for their cause. For the opposition to match this effort with money was too expensive even for the richest of the rich. The boycott that these families could sustain in the face of impossible odds was successful because they had always been forced to live and become self-sufficient at sustaining their meager existence under even harsher conditions. Big agribusiness was brought to its knees and signed labor agreements.

New Realities

The peaceful creation of new realities is always possible, as is the destruction of seemingly all-powerful evil empires. It is not always "how big is the dog in the fight"; many times it can become "how big is the fight in the dog." It can also become "how smart is the underdog." Think of Gandhi against the British Empire in India or Nelson Mandela versus the South African white regime, who had to fight from a prison cell for twenty-seven years and came out a winner and the first black president of South Africa.

Today's Relevance

But a far more relevant point was that a small force could take on a large, powerful force and, through skill in the art of war and conflict, defeat or frustrate the superior adversary. Whereas my grandfather advised me as an undersized football player that if my heart was big enough, I was big enough, I now must modify that statement because we are operating outside the protected confines of the football stadium with its structured, level playing field and officials. Now, in the real world, a more appropriate rendition is this: if my heart is big enough, if my experience and plan smart enough, and my perseverance tough enough, then it is possible for me to successfully take on any adversary, no matter how big and powerful.

How and Why Large, Powerful Organizations Protect Their Interest

President John F. Kennedy said that the United States had no eternal friends and allies, only eternal interests. Countries and corporations are primarily concerned with protecting their vested interest to protect and further the financial and property interest of their citizens and shareholders. These requirements are imposed by law, and officers and directors must account for and explain their actions in this regard.

It was my understanding of what I call the *iron law of vested interest* that caused me to lose my faith in intellectualism. As a student, I would engage in intellectual conversations with well-educated classmates concerning the problems of the world and society. Then it dawned on me that the fundamental assumptions of our conversations were that once we could agree on "the right thing," as rational beings, we would do what reason told us to do. I was confronted with what was then a Whittier College truism. John Herman Randall's book, *The Making of the Modern Mind*, contained the statement, "Man is a rational animal, but his animalism is more deeply rooted than his rationality, he cannot live by truth alone." What if your family's fortune was in steel, and your conversations convinced you that the companies competing against your family's interests were right in switching to and tying up all supplies of, carbon? As a rational person, are you going to lie down to the carbon interest or are you going to find a way to protect your family's steel interest, whether or not it still makes sense? We were wasting time arguing about reason; economic interest would rule the day.

Benjamin Franklin said, "If you would persuade, speak of interest, not of reason."

But examining the nature and the vested interest of countries and corporate business entities, I found an even more powerful group of potential adversaries.

Robert Michaels, in his nineteenth-century study of Italian Socialist labor unions, *Political Parties*, refers to what he called the "The Iron Law of Oligarchy." Michaels was part of what were referred to as "the heirs of Machiavelli," students of the intricacies and workings of powerful political entities. He observed that large, powerful interests would inevitably concentrate over time into oligarchies, a few at the top that ran everything. They cut across national borders and were primarily economic interests that would recruit and control the political leaders.

Gaetano Mosca was a contemporary of Robert Michaels and held to the theory that all politics was a competition between elite minorities vying for power. The masses of people were not involved in politics. They let the elites fight for power, which to them was only remotely relevant to the issues they faced daily and that determined the conduct of their lives. I found this interesting because, in creating a political machine in high school, we had conducted a sociological study of the student body and found that after we had identified all the groups and clicks, they only amounted to 15 percent of the student body. Most students belonged to what we called the nameless that were just there to vegetate. However, these nameless amorphous elements accounted for 85 percent of the votes. So, we ignored the vocal clicks that got most of the public attention and concentrated on securing the support of the nobodies. The machine we founded stayed in control of student politics for years after we graduated. We found that elections are determined by the nobodies. They were passive but all powerful. A genius of American democracy is that the elites must cater to the nobodies to remain in power.

Armed with this knowledge of how powerful entities are motivated and why they operate as they do, I was prepared to devise strategies to counter and influence their conduct toward my interest. Two of the most important strategies I have found useful will now be described.

1. Powerful adversaries generally have other powerful enemies. If the enemy of my adversary is potentially my ally, I would look for ways to form working alliances. This generally took the form of putting together blocks of votes at conventions where the giants would vie for power but where my small block was just enough to put one or the other over the top. I would form an alliance with my adversary's enemy, and together, we would prevail. I encountered similar situations in business and in financial campaigns to secure control of companies and markets.

2. I refer to the following as the Samson tactic. The story of Samson and Delilah is the biblical account of the world's strongest man. He was betrayed by his love for Delilah, who knew his vulnerabilities and weakened him so that his enemies could capture and blind him, burning out his eyes while he was in a weakened condition. In time, his strength returned, and seeking to bring down his adversaries in the court, he requested to be placed next to the structural pillars that sat on the foundation holding up the arena where his enemies in the court would be seated. When all were present, he rose to attempt to push aside the supporting pillar. All in attendance mocked him for attempting an impossible feat. Then, in a mighty second effort, the pillar fell, the arena collapsed, and he and all his enemies were killed.

    I found that when confronted with unfairness by a large entity, I would not fight the unfair actions, because they were masters at justifying arbitrary action and always were favored by the deciding tribunal. So instead, I would search for the foundation of their entire organization, claim it was not legitimate, and attempt to bring down the entire empire. In one case, it was a dispute over $300,000 in pension funds from a system managing more than $50 billion in pension capital. I found a vulnerability that I threatened to exploit. The chances of my being successful were probably less than 1 percent but not totally impossible. They were then confronted with the choice of taking the 1 percent chance that they could lose everything, or take no chance by giving my client $300,000, which was nothing to them. They paid over immediately so that they did not have to take even a 1 percent chance, because for them, the possibility represented by that small danger was enormous, and they could buy their way out for a pittance.

I witnessed a variation on this when I was chairman of the board of a national bank. There were 350 banks in the state. An attorney sued all 350 banks on some obscure claim and then offered to settle with each bank for $1,000. It would cost the banks $5,000 to answer and another $15,000 to litigate. He did this for three years straight. Each year, the board of directors would curse and whine about the unfairness but then would vote to pay him the $1,000. That meant that the banks paid $1,000 each, and the attorney who sued pocketed $350,000 each year because it was too expensive to take him on in court.

LESSON 7
Solutions in Personal Effectiveness

Time is valuable. It is not to be squandered. An old Mexican proverb says that time that is lost causes even the saints to cry. The most effective thing we can do is use our time well.

How many times have your started the day with the best of intentions and realized by late afternoon that you haven't been able to get anything important done, and now the evening's obligations will take what is left of your time? When the pressure in on to get something done, it can be a miserable feeling. How many times have you felt that you had no control over using your time well?

I was helped a great deal in this respect by a professor I met at a conference at a Midwestern university in 1968. Periodically, I find it useful to review what I learned and how I added to it. What follows are a few relevant concepts.

Beware of overload. It is a disease of organizations and leaders. Leaders tend to take on more than they can do and, additionally, to let friends, relatives, and those in need throw responsibilities on them. Young leaders are often intelligent, arrogant, and full of pride. They are flattered and can't say no. They feel they can do anything. They don't realize that some people make a career out of getting other people to do the hard work for them. Time is a limited resource. The effective leader needs to get the important work done first, but those who are exploiting only care about their own projects and push the leader away from the work that is important to their success. These time vampires can do great damage. A leader with character and not overly narcissistic will recognize the danger and learn to say no.

I should point out, however, there are cases where relationships or past obligations would not permit my saying no, and I learned to avoid situations where I would have to say no. I took care not to let these situations arise. I could not say no to my immediate family or to friends who had helped me when I was in real need. Because my needs were great, I had many such friends. It had to be really important for them to make the effort needed to corner me so that they could make a request. Whenever I allowed myself to get cornered, it cost me time and effectiveness.

Professional Work versus Political Work

It is important to understand the difference between professional work and political work. To get professional work done requires time alone without interruptions. Professional productivity is generally required to create products that can be sold for revenue. No productivity, no product, no money. Interruptions kill productivity. One needs to be truly ruthless when engaged in professional work. I sometimes put a sign outside my door that says I have been cancelled until a specific date, when I will emerge to talk to people, and barring a life-and-death emergency, my door stays closed. When people call, I don't answer. I am not there.

Political work is different. It is all interruptions. It is making contacts, negotiating deals, networking, selling, and all things that are more effective when done in person.

The problem is that your best people are generally your best at both. But professional work and political work are not compatible. You must do one or the other. Trying to do both results in someone being shortchanged. I find that I must schedule days for just professional work and avoid interruptions and schedule other days when I do only political work and don't even try to get to professional work. Employers make the mistake of putting the best people in peripheral jobs, where they have contact with the public because they are good at that, but then expect them to do professional work and meet deadlines because they are the best at that. The employee is then only marginally effective at either.

They must be protected from interruptions to get professional work done.

Let us consider interruptions. The three most disruptive interruptions are telephone calls, walk-in unscheduled visitors, and meetings. Texting has been useful in avoiding telephone interruptions. One can now wait until time is set aside for short-range tasks to answer text messages. Never answer the phone when doing professional work. Turn the phone off. I once asked a woman who refused to answer the phone, "What if it is important?" She said that if it is important, then they would certainly call back. Lock the door on walk-in visitors, leaving a sign to make an appointment at times that you set aside for meeting people. Meetings can be a great time waster. Like Murphy's law that says if anything can possibly go wrong, it will, there is a law for meetings that says that the time a meeting will consume will expand to fill the time allotted for it. Meetings are supposed to get business done, but they can turn into periods for griping and emotional adjustment. If the participants get right to it, they can generally get their decisions made within a half hour. So rather than scheduling a meeting from nine to noon, schedule it at 11:30 a.m. so that if people want to stay longer, it is cutting into their lunchtime. If three hours are available, it will take three hours, but if only a half hour is available, participants tend to find a way to get the essential work done within the half hour. If there are complaints that more time is needed, schedule it at 11:15 a.m. whether or not all the participants are present.

The Organization of Tasks and Time

Socrates observed that the unexamined life is not worth living. A greater loss is that the unplanned day will squander an irretrievable portion of one's life. Time that is lost causes even the saints to cry is a Mexican expression. As a youth, I ignored this. Young people tend to feel that they will live forever. Kipling's poem "If" states, "If you can fill the unforgiving minute / With sixty seconds' worth of distance run, / Yours is the Earth and everything that's in it." Today, I value every second and plan every minute for sixty seconds worth of production.

To be effective and not lose time tomorrow, it is important to plan your day the night before. It is useful to divide tasks into three categories: short-term that will take less than an hour, intermediate-term that will take more than an hour and up to three hours to complete, and long-term that will take more than three hours to complete.

You need to make a list of all the tasks you need to do. You must prioritize them and divide the high-priority tasks into short-term, intermediate-term, and long-term. You then must schedule them into your day. Give priority to the intermediate tasks, not the short-term ones. There is a natural tendency to do the short-term ones first, cross them off your list and feel that you are accomplishing something. Short-term tasks are seldom that important. Do these during breaks and after finishing an intermediate work session. It is the intermediate tasks (one to three hours) that must be a priority. It is in these periods that we get done most things that make us feel that we have accomplished something. Most people are fresh with great creativity for this period. Completion of these tasks should be your priority. Get these done first, and you will begin to see effective production. Fill in blank time with the short-term tasks. The long-term tasks need to be subdivided into intermediate tasks that are completed within the two- or three-hour sessions. There are four times of the day when one can schedule a three-hour session, early morning before breakfast, the morning between breakfast and lunch, the afternoon before dinner, and the evening hours can also be used. Although four periods of the day may be available in theory, most people consider themselves fortunate if they can find time to schedule or be productive in one or two.

Understand that it is important to honor your physiology. Some people are full of creativity and energy in the morning. Others are like zombies that can't wake up until after the second cup of coffee at about eleven in the morning. Some people are asleep by nine o'clock, and others are very creative between eleven at night and two in the morning. It is important that you schedule your working sessions at times when you are creative and have energy.

Then you make appointments to work and cut off interruptions during these time periods. You now have set aside time to be productive, and your effectiveness multiplies. Be sure to follow your priorities and not those of others. Do not let other people burden you with their problems and priorities. Yours come first, and there really is no time for anything else. There are more of your own than you will have time to deal with. Realize that only some of your priorities will be addressed because there is never enough time.

One can divide priorities from level 1 to level 5. Level 1 priorities are those that can be life-threatening, such as breathing, eating, clothing, shelter, and so on. Level 2 priorities are vital to your business, career, education, and life's work. Level 3 priorities and useful but not vital. Level 4 priorities are important to others but not to you. Level 5 priorities are only to be done when everything else is done.

Level 1 and 2 priorities should be done before you worry about any other lower priorities. Your effectiveness depends on being effective at getting the Level 1 and 2 priorities completed well. Until they are done, nothing else should matter or be given a thought.

It is also important to understand the difference between vital and urgent. It sounds like they are similar, but they are not. It is a source of confusion that needs to be understood. Vital is a level 1 priority. If you don't take care of it, you will die. Vital is always important. Urgent means calling for immediate action. It may refer to something vital but not necessarily.

A person may come to your office demanding immediate attention to a level 3 priority item. It may be urgent, calling for immediate attention, but it may be for something that is not vital but only convenient. Don't let others put their low-priority urgency monkeys on your back, especially while you are dealing with vital issues, which is all the time.

It is vital to engage in next-day planning and congruent behavior. Congruent behavior furthers progress toward achieving your goals. All your activity during the day should be congruent with furthering your goals. Otherwise, you are wasting time.

A great danger is a distraction that results in the loss of a block of time during the morning or afternoon. This disrupts momentum and results in the effective loss of day's productivity. What is the value of a day? The loss of time, limited as it is on this planet, is so tragic that even saints mourned its loss. Don't get sidetracked during the day. Be aware of your momentum and don't lose it by getting sidetracked.

When leading a group that has been put together for their creativity, there is a way to get the most out of what they have to offer. It was developed by experts at NASA, I am told. Get them to a table and give them the problem, proposition, or question to be considered. Ask them not to discuss it but to start writing down the points they would make to address it. Then after about twenty minutes, take up the papers. Studies have found that about 40 percent more ideas emerge by doing this. Ordinarily, discussion stifles this creativity. By writing it out before the discussion, ideas do not get buried.

LESSON 8
Generic Business Franchise

Why is the franchise concept important? The answer is in the statistics. According to the United States Small Business Administration, 50 percent of business start-ups go under within two years of their founding, and 80 percent within five years. A new business owner's chances of surviving beyond year five are about 20 percent. A franchise operation, however, will be successful 95 percent of the time. Only 5 percent a year will fail. To increase the odds for small and minority business success, we studied what aspects of franchises gave them their success.

We isolated seven disciplines that a franchise provides that small businesspersons are usually lacking. We then attempted to research procedures and resources that could be marshalled and came up with the following:

1. Accounting and bookkeeping
2. Planning
3. Finance
4. Marketing and sales
5. Personnel
6. Regulatory compliance
7. Public relations

1. Accounting and bookkeeping

When I became the executive director of a small government-funded minority business association in the 1970s, I found that many small business owners ignore accounting capabilities such as score keeping, accurate data for problem recognition, and implications suggesting problem-solving solutions. I found that the typical small business only concerns itself with accounting twice a year, when they must prepare tax returns and when they need a loan from a bank and the bank requests their financial statements. Otherwise, bookkeeping is just an unpleasant nuisance with which they would rather not bother.

They tend to toss all their receipts into a bag or a shoebox and do a haphazard job of maintaining their checkbook stubs that tells them when, why, and to whom they paid money. I found that their accountants spent a great deal of valuable time doing research to fill in all the missing blanks, trying to get the books in order. As a result, when they requested accounting services, the accounts would reply, "I can't get to it until after tax season, and it will take anywhere from two weeks to two months to prepare reasonably accurate and reliable financial statements." For many of these businesses, a two-month delay on financing would put them out of business.

We decided to find a solution for this small business curse. We made it the first and highest priority. Following a tip from an accountant on what he would need to prepare statements, I wrote a spreadsheet program that would create an income statement and a trial balance. I even wrote an algorithm that would find the error when the accounts did not balance. We then started an education program, telling our clients that we could work miracles, provided they incorporate the following procedures. We prepared a chart of accounts using as a guide the categories set out in IRS Schedule C, Profit or Loss from Operation of a Business or Profession. At the very least, our statements would always produce relevant information for tax preparation. Armed with a chart of accounts, we then created two short sentences to guide them. These were, "You can't write a check until you have paid the Nag. Also, whenever money comes in, you have to get

GASD." This meant that you had to record five pieces of information whenever you wrote a check. These were:

P = The payee you are paying
D = The check date
N = The check number
A = The amount of the check
G = The general ledger code account number

PD-NAG = Paid Nag, which everyone could understand

When money came in, it was necessary to record four pieces of information:

G = The general ledger code account number
A = The amount of money that was received
S = The source of the money
D = The date it came in

GASD—everybody loves to get GASD.

With this information on hand, the accountants could do their work. But we took it a step further. The small business client would make an appointment and come in at 8:00 a.m. with the records. We would split up the work to do the data entry and run it through the spreadsheet. Typically, the income statement and the trial balance would be ready before noon the same day. Because word got around about the time advantage, everyone learned to Pay the Nag and get GASD. Accounting became relevant to them.

Today, there are several bookkeeping programs available. Two that stand out are QuickBooks at the low end and Net Suites at the high end. But if you have faithfully Paid the Nag and gotten GASD appropriately, any accounting system along with your accountant will have what they need to produce your financial statements in a timely manner.

2. Planning

Few entrepreneurs have had any formal instruction in planning. Typically, prior to obtaining a loan guaranteed by the Small Business Administration, a business plan setting forth the work program and financial assumptions and projections must be submitted.

When seeking equity participations from investors, the elements of an offering circular or private placement memorandum will include elements from the business plan. These include the work program, résumés and qualifications of the managing personnel, a complete list of risk factors that may be encountered, along with the financial assumptions upon which the financial projections for the venture were based.

These procedures, however, still lead to an 80 percent failure rate. Why? Two books that I have recently encountered seem to tell the story. The first is entitled *Burn the Business Plan*, and its premise is that research has established that business plans are only useful when seeking funding. They are required by the funding sources such as the Small Business Administration and the participating bank or other lender receiving the government guarantee. It is stated that once wartime hostilities begin, the first casualty is the plan of battle. Plans and assumptions fall apart quickly during the heat of battle. The same is true of small business operations. Research has shown that business plans have very little to do with making a business a success. Furthermore, some of your most successful businesses started without a business plan.

The second book is probably the most important book on small business ever written. It is entitled *The E-Myth Revisited, Why Small Businesses Fail and What to Do About It* (*The E-Myth Revisited: Why Most Small Businesses Don't Work and What to Do About It by Michael E. Gerber*). The first half of this book should be mandatory reading for anyone contemplating starting a business. It is an excellent presentation of what happens to most inexperienced entrepreneurs and how and why they fail. If they still determine to start a business, then the second half of the book becomes mandatory reading.

It is curious that I came up with the concept of the generic business franchise in 1977, the same year that the *E-Myth* book with its promotion of the franchise prototype was published. Apparently, we both came up with similar notions about the same time. One main difference was that I wrote a three-page summary of my observations and notions, while the other author did serious research as to origins and elements of franchises and wrote a masterpiece of more than 250 pages.

Whereas this book is about the nuts and bolts of how to be a leader, the *E-Myth* book is about the nuts and bolts of how to create a franchise prototype. It represents planning on steroids. It is very much about how to make the business a success. It ignores funding and proceeds to the how and why of creating a successful enterprise.

3. Finance

Finance is not just about finding someone who will lend or invest a lot of money with you. In many ways, it is like a learned profession. There are eternal and shifting rules for both equity and debt financing. Implementing these rules requires a keen knowledge of the reasons behind the rule. Once you know finance, however, you will know how to secure the capital you need to start and operate your business.

Some useful background follows. A report issued by the Federal Reserve Bank in 1974 stated that the budget of the US federal government was $108 billion. The total for all state and local governments was $104 billion. All public pension funds and all insurance companies had assets of $23 billion and $27 billion respectfully. The value of all the American households, however, was more than $1.7 trillion. American household represented the greatest concentration of wealth ever assembled.

All this wealth represented sources for aggregating capital. Capital is wealth used for the creation of more wealth. Because of inflation, if one has wealth and does not invest it, it loses value by the rate of inflation each year. As one millionaire said, "I have $50,000,000, but inflation is running at 10 percent a year. If I don't invest it, in five years it will lose 50 percent of its buying power and be worth $25,000,000. Do you realize that I will have lost $25,000,000?"

People with wealth need to put it to work by investing it. Credit rating agencies rate various investment instruments like stocks, which represent equity ownership in a company, and bonds, which are debt instruments generally in the form of corporate promissory notes. Those instruments with a high rating of triple-b or better are considered reasonably safe for investment and are considered "investment grade." Fiduciaries who invest other people's money are only authorized to invest in investment grade securities. They breach their fiduciary duty if they invest in instruments that are not considered investment grade by the major credit-rating agencies. Instruments with a lower credit rating that are not investment grade are considered junk and require paying a higher return because of the increased risk they represent. Because many have paid off, junk bonds are now referred to by some as high yield bonds.

When a bank takes in deposits and needs to lend the money to earn interest income, it is investing in its borrowers. When is a borrower a good investment? One of the first lessons when I started a career as a businessperson was that commercial banks and insurance companies were not in the business of taking risk. If they perceived any risk, they ruled out any involvement. They will only lend or insure if it appears that there is no risk whatsoever. Bankers are interested in borrowers who can use credit, not those who need credit.

The theory used to be to only lend to those borrowers who demonstrate the three Cs. These are character, collateral, and capacity. Are you a person of good character who pays your bills? In addition, can you put up collateral so that if you have a misfortune, it is not the bank's misfortune? Finally, if you get into trouble, do you have the capacity to get out of it so that the bank doesn't have to bother with collections? Later, cash was added to the requirements so that the bank only lends to people who don't need it unless you have a government guarantee. Enter the Small Business Administration (SBA) who guarantees 90 percent of a loan to a qualified borrower and the Federal Housing Administration (FHA) that guarantees mortgages for home buyers unable to qualify for conventional financing.

As banking has become more automated, these human tendencies have been replaced by computer formulas and credit scores. Few branch managers today have any lending authority. Central offices manage the computers running the lending business. Recently, laws have been changed to permit high interest rates for loans made by private lenders who make loans that were once the market of commercial banks. Credit cards pay an increasing role in financing business capital.

Companies that appear to be successful and have high credit ratings go public (sell their stock to the public) with the assistance of investment bankers who manage IPOs (initial public offerings).

Small company private placements are managed by small investment banking broker-dealers and by private issuers who operate using exemptions to the securities laws. This can be a source of private capital, but it can be extremely risky and lead to criminal charges because the exact requirements of the exemption were not complied with, despite every effort to do so. You must make full disclosure of all possible risk factors. If you inadvertently overlook one or more, it works as a strict liability. Either you comply with the subjective requirements of full disclosure where neither best efforts nor reasonable efforts are enough, either you comply exactly to a subjective standard, or you're a criminal.

How to Finance Your Business

When bankers, acting as natural persons, were in control of operating the banking industry, thing were much different than they are today. Today, artificial intelligence, as the logic language of computers, uses algorithms to make decisions. It is now possible to establish business credit without ever being reviewed or evaluated by a human. Your author has done it the old-fashioned people way and now functions in the modern computer-dominated environment. To knowledgeable practitioners, both can be effective.

In the old days and still viable today, early capital comes from friends and family. The key is to create an entity that meets the credit qualifications for debt and to have equity investors who are accredited investors. An accredited investor is a person who has a million dollars in assets, not counting their home. Accredited investors are exempt from most aspects of the securities laws, but you still must provide them with full disclosure of all risk factors.

Two ways of starting a business have proved successful. First is to learn the business and gain experience by working in someone else's business until you are ready to go out on your own. Avoid what can be an expensive education by letting someone else finance your learning experiences. The second recommendation is to begin by developing an income-producing enterprise on a small level, where experience is less costly; then scale it up. Your business must produce income, or you don't have a business. If your business cannot make it without money, it probably can't make it with money. I have seen people create what appears to be cashflow but is really a debt-based Ponzi scheme. I have seen real estate entrepreneurs live from mortgage loan to mortgage loan and appear to have money. If inflation continues to push up the property's appraised value, they can borrow and give the illusion of making money until the next down market causes a crash.

Sources for information on qualifying for debt financing include going to your neighborhood bank and asking them for their policies on lending. Who do they lend to and do you qualify? The Small Business Administration is another good source.

For the rules on taking money from equity partners, see the Securities and Exchange Commission's small business finance webpage. Consult Google for your state's blue skies law requirements for the private issue of securities. Even with qualified legal counsel, this can be a very dangerous area to work in because the laws on securities fraud, unlike common-law fraud, are not based on Scienter, a legal term meaning "intent to deceive," but rather on technical issues involved in meeting the exact requirements of exemptions to the law. Situations can arise that make exact compliance effectively impossible. In practice, it is a form of criminal strict liability. Because criminal statutes are involved, if something goes wrong (even if it was unintentional), you are a criminal because you did not meet the exact requirements of the exemption. For most small businesspeople, dealing in securities is not wise.

One firm I work with as a business consultant that can be effective in the modern-day environment is Letstalkbusinesstoday.com. They prepare documents that fulfill the legal requirements for initiating business operations. Furthermore, they are familiar with old-school protocols and modern computer requirements. They can navigate the sometimes treacherous and troubled sea of financial underwriting and know how to overcome barriers to financial liquidity.

4. Marketing and sales

Traditionally, marketing was the strategy for achieving sales, while sales was the art practiced by professional salespeople. Marketing personnel would create a strategy to successfully reach and create sales leads and then send in the sales personnel to engage with the prospects and close sales.

Today, this model has been replaced by professional marketing organizations that use demographics and psychographics. Demographics are the group that marketers advertise to after researching who will buy and why. Psychographics tell you why they buy. These marketing principles and research methods are sophisticated and enable the capability to accurately predict the level of sales that will be achieved. You can now prepare a sales budget, sign an advertising contract, and know in advance what will be your revenue.

Without access to budgets for the modern marketing research and advertising materials, nor the funds to train a professional sales force, we have gone in a separate direction.

Our system came out of a realization that prospective salespersons dislike being rejected and wish to avoid being told no when they ask for the sale. We followed a different path designed to have the prospect tell us that they want to buy.

We refer to it as problem recognition sales. We provide facts that assist the prospect to recognize that they have a problem that needs an immediate solution. Our product is the solution of choice, and they ask if we will sell it to them.

5. Personnel and human resource development

Three issues are key to personnel: labor laws, motivation, and systems to achieve performance.

All states have labor laws with which all businesses must comply.

Use a search engine for information on how to comply. The issue is how to comply while simultaneously implementing your procedures for motivation and performance. You need to prevent conflicts.

The Hersey and Blanchard material on situational leadership has grown out of decades of research and producing useful educational materials concerning motivation and performance (*Management of Organizational Behavior: Leading Human Resources,* 8th ed., by Paul Hersey, Kenneth H. Blanchard, Dewey E. Johnson, https://www.amazon.com/exec/obidos/ASIN/0130175986/changingminds-20).

However, one of the most intriguing methods is referred to as *The People System,* set forth in the *E-Myth* book (*The E-Myth Revisited: Why Most Small Businesses Don't Work and What to Do About It* by Michael E. Gerber).

I recommend consulting with all three sources before deciding on how you approach this subject. I have found personnel issues to be the most difficult part of running a business.

6. Regulatory compliance

Use a search engine to locate the business start-up requirements in your jurisdiction. Remember to search labor laws, state and federal tax compliance, workmen's compensation insurance, equipment licenses, annual reports, insurance coverage, and so on.

7. Public relations

Simple clarity in communications is a key to public relations. Develop a simple and direct mission statement stating who you are, what you do, and why the public should care. Develop inexpensive methods of communicating, such as press releases supported by a press packet. (See also books like *Branding on a Shoestring* by Kim Speed, http://brandingonashoestringbook.com/.)

A Word of Caution

Recently, some franchises are beginning to show signs of wear and decline. Whether or not the franchise concept continues in vogue, the need for rigorous, detailed planning will always remain a requirement and hallmark of effective leadership.

The Political Implications and Dangers of Overplanning

One source I encountered years ago spoke of middle managers who used planning to control their superiors. About a decade ago, I came up against adversaries who were very good at it and who had impeccable credentials.

In Gerber's *E-Myth* book, the proposed franchise prototype is essentially a play where everyone has predetermined lines to read and act out. The purpose is to remove all discretion from the employee. The product that is being sold is not a commodity such as a hamburger but the experience. When a customer goes into a franchise establishment, they expect to have the same experience that they found so pleasing on their prior visit. The well-managed franchise will deliver the experience again and satisfy the customer's expectation.

The planners, who essentially wrote the play, have a great deal of power and are not necessarily averse to using it for their own benefit. They can overplan in such a way that they not only remove all discretion from the employees but also from organization executives and managers, who should be the ones authorized to make decision based upon their judgment and discretion.

The planners write a script that predecides matters that they see, or hope to foresee, will arise in the future. They write the outcome, so that they decide the issue to their advantage long before it ever comes to the attention of senior management. Since the entire play was initially approved by the board of directors, any deviation is against company policy, putting the senior manager in the uncomfortable position of defying the board of directors or following his or her judgment. Typically, at this point, the planners are protecting their position by discretely sabotaging the senior manager. The middle management planners control their superiors through discretely organized ambushes that make it easier for all just to follow the approved script and let the planners have their way.

Other Approaches for Emerging Businesses

The System of the *Nina*, the *Pinta*, and the *Santa Maria*
versus That of the *Titanic*:
An Alternate to Crossing the Chasm
for a New Enterprise

Summary of *Crossing the Chasm*
Geoffrey A. Moore, *Crossing the Chasm, Marketing and Selling High-Tech Products to Mainstream Customer* (revised edition), HarperCollins Publishers, New York, 1999.

The initiation of a business venture acts to place it directly in what Geoffrey Moore refers to as the chasm. The chasm is an unpleasant place in which to dwell. It is full of the business equivalent of mountains, canyons, deserts, and seas that are loaded with land mines, underwater mines, submerged boulders, bandits, and pirates, where resources are exhausted, customers make unreasonable demands, competitors issue vicious, untrue rumors of your allegedly inadequate products, where meeting payroll gets harder and harder, and the business organization is constantly challenged with overcoming frustrations and must constantly face the specter of real and imagined failure, a constant companion in the chasm.

Moore's book is based upon the experience of high-tech companies in Silicon Valley that are launched with what is perceived to be adequate capital.

In my view, they are like the *Titanic* steam ship that was designed to be unsinkable until the frailty of human capability shows that there are always factors that are unanticipated. Even with gigantic accumulations of capital and human and logistical resources, success cannot be guaranteed.

Can a small venture with only a small amount of capital successfully cross the chasm to business success?

The Explorer-Colony Approach

Using the explorer-colony approach, all that is needed are the resources to establish just one small self-sufficient colony that can grow and create two more, each with the same capability. The seeds of an evil empire's destruction can emerge out of the good elements within it.

Nature provides the example of exponential growth. By just establishing one such colony, each offspring and their offspring can then double and double to grow into more than a million within fewer than thirty iterations.

Self-sufficiency is the key. With it, the burn rate, which is the rate at which capital is being consumed, becomes irrelevant. Self-sufficiency can replace millions of dollars in accumulated capital and still produce superior results. Nature starts with just one cell and grows quickly into millions. If you can duplicate nature's capability, you don't need millions of dollars in capital. This can be a limiting factor, especially within one's psyche. The idea that your business can only get big if it has big money to start with is a fallacy. If you can design a product that in effect duplicates its numbers with each iteration, then you can start with a penny and be over a million dollars within thirty iterations. In theory, you can start really small and be in the millions within a month.

Fifteenth- and sixteenth-century explorers, such as Columbus sailing to the Americas in the tiny forty-foot vessels, the *Nina*, the *Pinta*, and the *Santa Maria*, depended upon finding life-giving resources from the environment. These were sailing vessels that had to be self-sufficient and capable of foraging island and ocean resources to fulfill their missions. A self-sufficient vessel, capable of marathon voyages, can travel for months at a time to faraway locations to establish colonies. These colonies can then begin to develop and support new additional colonies. The idea is to grow them so that they grow exponentially. Each produces the resources to establish and equip two additional colonies, which are also designed to develop and transfer the same capabilities. Additional resources from home base are not necessary. Each colony generates its own capability to double its growth. This capability is part of each colony's DNA design that is transferred to each new colony. They then grow to the point where joint colonial action becomes feasible. The birth of the United States is an example.

Individual self-sufficient businesses can be created and sustained, and they can enable a venture to successfully cross the chasm using similar strategies.

Once established, each of these businesses can continue indefinitely. Not only do they eliminate the primary cause of small business failure, but they can create and sustain small businesses so that they can grow into big business that can take on the established power structures and create a new paradigm of wealth, health, and widespread happiness and well-being.

Securities Laws

There is an enormous danger that generally goes unappreciated by new ventures. This danger lurks within the enforcement of securities laws. These laws are all inclusive and are an exception to constitutional protections of due process in their enforcement.

The federal government and most states regulate the investment of money into businesses. Most people are surprised to learn that the basic rule is that a business is not allowed to accept investment money from passive investors unless they have registered with the federal government's Securities and Exchange Commission and have an offering circular approved by the government issued to them before they accept money. For the exact same transaction, they must also have permission at the state level—in California, for example, a permit from the Corporations Commission or Department of Business Oversite to issue and sell participations in investments. If they do not, they commit a crime by selling an unregistered security without a permit to do so. They commit a separate crime if they fail to provide full disclosure of the risk to which the investor will be subjecting the funds and all information concerning the venture and its management. Good faith effort is not a defense. Common-law Scienter, intent to deceive, which is necessary to establish common-law fraud, is not required to establish securities fraud. If you make an honest good faith effort to do it right and make a mistake or leave out something inadvertently, you're a criminal and a felon under both the federal and state law. You have broken laws within each of these jurisdictions.

All you did is take money from an investor. So why aren't almost all small business people in jail? There seem to be two principal reasons, exemptions and selective enforcement.

Exemptions

The laws include several exemptions for which many businesses believe they are eligible. Among the most important are the private placement exemption and other safe harbor exemptions included within the statutes. At the federal level, the important ones are at Section 4(2) and 4(6) of the Securities and Exchange Act of 1933 and the regulations promulgated thereto, especially Regulation D. These are all covered in the small business finance section of the SEC webpage. Similarly, in California, Corporation Code Section 25,102 contains the exemptions, and it is important to note 25,102 (h), (f), and (n). It is amazing how creative prosecutors can be at finding loopholes that destroy qualifications that a businessperson believed would protect them.

Selective Enforcement

These laws are enforced in a very technical way. Failure to dot one *i* or cross a *t* can land you in jail. Either you comply exactly, not reasonably but exactly, with the requirements of the exemptions or you have committed a felony.

In practice, I have found that it is nearly impossible to comply, no matter how hard one tries; there is almost always a flaw that can kill the exemption. If the enforcement officials want to enforce every violation, most small business owners would be in jail. It is too big a job, but that works in favor of the enforcement officials.

They have potent tools when there is a problem. If everything goes well and no one loses any money, no one cares or raises any issues. Nothing happens.

However, we noted above that the Small Business Administration says that 80 percent of business start-ups will fail within five years. This means that someone's money will be lost 80 percent of the time. Most small businesses, however, do not have the sophistication to do a securities offering. It is only when one attempts one and fails that some investor may complain. Sometimes they understand the issues that led to failure and do not complain. Until they complain to law enforcement, no one seems to care. When they do complain, the amount involved by an individual investor is so small that it does not meet the law enforcement agency's priorities for taking action because bigger, more important issues must take a higher priority for an agency with limited resources.

I have noticed that a quirk of human nature is that when investors make money, they believe that it was because they were smart investors. When they lose money, it is because the promoter was a crook, no matter how hard they tried to do it right.

When the investors begin to complain to enforcement officials, these officials have potent tools with which to give the investors their pound of flesh. They do this by going after the innocent, well-meaning promoter who happened to be unlucky. Many lives, especially those of minority entrepreneurs, have been ruined in this fashion. I have seen them give their best efforts, work very hard, and sacrifice all they have, and still the business fails, and they lose investors' money. They find out very soon and in very vivid fashion that no good deed goes unpunished.

Also, I have noticed that it is not uncommon for public officials to call upon enforcement agents to help cripple an opposition leader by going after alleged violations of the securities laws. As one once told me, what good is power if you can't abuse it? I have seen cases developed and prosecuted in ways that resemble framing an innocent person with false evidence or evidence secured illegally.

If you are in business, you want to avoid making enemies, especially those with friends in high places or those with powerful capabilities. There are hidden legal vulnerabilities out there that can be unfairly, illegally, and deceptively used against anyone and with great effect.

LESSON 9
Internet Marketing, Making Money Today, and the Gig Economy

The internet is making great changes in the business landscape. At the local small business level, most of the rules set forth above about franchise concepts, "crossing the chasm," and securities laws are still very relevant and will hold true for some time. But the internet is disrupting certain aspects of business.

In many ways, in its early stages, the internet has brought real competition to American capitalism. Google and YouTube have leveled the playing field and made logistics a lot easier for mom and pop. Amazon and Walmart, not to mention Home Depot and Lowes, have changed business procurement. Debit cards, credit cards, PayPal, eBay, and Craigslist have changed payment and procurement. Banking is better and worse. Real estate today is an internet business.

The landscape is unrecognizable from fifteen years ago. What is clear to me is that few of the changes that have occurred were the ones that were expected to occur.

I remember back in 1957 when the top white male singers were Elvis Presley and Pat Boone. Boone was the favorite of the white establishment and retained some of the attributes of singers in the thirties and forties. Elvis was a white man signing like a black man and had learned much as a kid listening to music coming from the black clubs on Beale Street in Memphis, Tennessee. The conventional wisdom being promoted was that Elvis would fade and Pat Boone was the wave of the future. Rock and roll was under attack as the music of the devil. Then the Beatles and later New Kids on the Block came into prominence. All used the formula of having white signers sing black music. The more the establishment fought and ridiculed these performers, the more their popularity grew. The smart money was wrong.

Today, the biggest winner in my estimation is Jeff Bezos of Amazon. Everyone I knew predicted he would fail and ridiculed him constantly. He is now the richest man on the planet. I believe that he is just getting started.

There is a moment today when many entities are just marketing automated small businesses. One puts together a series of webpages and uses various forms of advertising to drive traffic to these landing pages, designed to give something in return for an email address. They then send automated communications through a funnel to establish a give-and-take rapport until the first of several sales is made. An attempt is made to create with each customer a long-term relationship so that future sales will occur. Strategically, the two key business issues are: what is the customer acquisition cost and what is the long-term value of the customer? There is an attempt to market affordable products initially but also eventually to sell relatively expensive products.

Once this point has been achieved, the idea is that through automation, the business runs itself, marketing to an audience of more than four billion internet users. The product fulfillment and payment tools are now in place to support these businesses.

Large-scale adjustments are occurring because of the internet not only for the big guys but for small business as well.

It will be persons who are able to adjust who will prosper in the new paradigm. Along these lines, an interesting analysis of neurolinguistic programming shows why adjustments are so difficult for many people. There is a programing that emanates from our family and is transferred automatically as we grow. It is said that this programming can be transferring concepts that were learned seven generations back. A generation is thought to be about thirty years, so today, many people are thinking about things that were learned about 1810. This learning reflects the values of that time and all the time that has passed since then.

When I think of that time, I think of Benjamin Franklin's letter essay to his son, called "The Way to Wealth," written on board a ship going to England in 1757. It included all the wisdom he had published over the years as the editor of *Poor Richard's Almanac*. It is also referred to as "Old Abraham's Speech" and is included as an addendum to this book. It praises the hard work and thrift of an agrarian society. One interesting comment was that in America, he had never seen a man die of starvation, but of overeating, a hundred thousand. That was in the 1700s, the eighteenth century.

In the nineteenth century, as America became industrialized, labor flowed to the factories for a job to support them in an urban environment. The values of the family then became much of the following: Be on time; don't be late to work. Be a good worker; get things done and don't talk and waste time. Dress like a good, clean, Christian gentlemen who will do his work and not make trouble. Do an honest day's work, don't cheat your boss, and you will earn an honest day's wages. All were the virtues of a good employee. People learned to think like an employee, adopted those values, and programmed them into the family without knowing it.

One of the problems of success in business is that the CEO entrepreneur is still thinking like an employee without realizing it. A key question of an employee is "How much does it cost?" A key question of a business investor is "What is my return on investment?" Employees and investor-entrepreneurs have different ways of thinking to be successful. In the nineteenth and twentieth centuries, "work hard, save, get educated, be dependable, persevere, and you will do all right" was gospel.

Internet Entrepreneurs

Having grown up in that environment, it is disorienting to hear internet entrepreneurs say they don't want to have to their lifestyle be driven by their business, like their parents did; they want an automated business that runs itself and produces sufficient cash to support their lifestyle. The work schedule with such a business is about four hours a week. This is considered all that is necessary to maintain it.

These entrepreneurs are constantly on the lookout for opportunities to create additional automated businesses. Ideally, they will always have about six or seven producing a total comfortable annual income of a few million dollars for them to afford the lifestyle of their preference.

The Gig Economy

There is a school of thought that says to call this the life of the millennials is baloney. Yes, there are a few successful businesspeople, as has always been the case, but most millennials today find that they live neither in the traditional employee environment nor an internet business environment. The agrarian economy, the industrial economy, and the information age—all are irrelevant. What we have today is a gig economy where everyone must hustle to get gigs (short-term jobs) to survive.

Alternate Economy Based on Self-Sufficient Homesteads

More reason to develop the alternate economy based on self-sufficient independent homestead estates is summarized and will be detailed in a future treatise. In a way, it is going back to our roots to recapture both a freedom and a power we as a people once had. It is like living a healthy life on a farm in the nineteenth century but with all the labor-saving devices and the communication channels that are available today. We are not then as susceptible to being powerless pawns in a world controlled by oligarchies. The independent homestead estate concept makes them irrelevant and allows us citizens to live our lives as a people in control of our own individual destinies.

Benjamin Franklin's "The Way to Wealth" (1758)

Courteous Reader, I have heard that nothing gives an author so great pleasure, as to find his works respectfully quoted by other learned authors.

This pleasure I have seldom enjoyed; for tho' I have been, if I may say it without vanity, an eminent author of almanacs annually now a full quarter of a century, my brother authors in the same way, for what reason I know not, have ever been very sparing in their applauses; and no other author has taken the least notice of me, so that did not my writings produce me some solid pudding, the great deficiency of praise would have quite discouraged me.

I concluded at length, that the people were the best judges of my merit; for they buy my works; and besides, in my rambles, where I am not personally known, I have frequently heard one or other of my adages repeated, with, as Poor Richard says, at the end on't; this gave me some satisfaction, as it showed not only that my instructions were regarded, but discovered likewise some respect for my authority; and I own, that to encourage the practice of remembering and repeating those wise sentences, I have sometimes quoted myself with great gravity. Judge then how much I must have been gratified by an incident I am going to relate to you.

I stopped my horse lately where a great number of people were collected at a vendue of merchant goods. The hour of sale not being come, they were conversing on the badness of the times, and one of the company called to a plain clean old man, with white locks,

"Pray, Father Abraham, what think you of the times? Won't these heavy taxes quite ruin the country? How shall we be ever able to pay them? What would you advise us to?"

Father Abraham stood up, and replied,

"If you'd have my advice, I'll give it you in short, for a word to the wise is enough, and many words won't fill a bushel, as Poor Richard says."

They joined in desiring him to speak his mind, and gathering round him, he proceeded as follows:

"Friends, says he, and neighbors, the taxes are indeed very heavy, and if those laid on by the government were the only ones we had to pay, we might more easily discharge them; but we have many others, and much more grievous to some of us.

We are taxed twice as much by our idleness, three times as much by our pride, and four times as much by our folly, and from these taxes the commissioners cannot ease or deliver us by allowing an abatement."

However, let us hearken to good advice, and something may be done for us; God helps them that help themselves, as Poor Richard says, in his almanac of 1733.

"It would be thought a hard government that should tax its people one tenth part of their time, to be employed in its service. But idleness taxes many of us much more, if we reckon all that is spent in absolute sloth, or doing of nothing, with that which is spent in idle employments or amusements, that amount to nothing.

Sloth, by bringing on diseases, absolutely shortens life.

Sloth, like rust, consumes faster than labor wears, while the used key is always bright, as Poor Richard says.

But dost thou love life, then do not squander time, for that's the stuff life is made of, as Poor Richard says.

How much more than is necessary do we spend in sleep! Forgetting that the sleeping fox catches no poultry, and that there will be sleeping enough in the grave, as Poor Richard says.

If time be of all things the most precious, wasting time must be, as Poor Richard says, the greatest prodigality, since, as he elsewhere tells us, lost time is never found again, and what we call time-enough, always proves little enough:

let us then be up and be doing, and doing to the purpose; so, by diligence shall we do more with less perplexity.

Sloth makes all things difficult, but industry all easy, as Poor Richard says; and he that riseth late, must trot all day, and shall scarce overtake his business at night.

While laziness travels so slowly, that poverty soon overtakes him, as we read in Poor Richard, who adds, drive thy business, let not that drive thee; and early to bed, and early to rise, makes a man healthy, wealthy and wise."

"So what signifies wishing and hoping for better times? We may make these times better if we bestir ourselves.

Industry need not wish, as Poor Richard says, and he that lives upon hope will die fasting.

There are no gains, without pains, then help hands, for I have no lands, or if I have, they are smartly taxed.

And, as Poor Richard likewise observes, he that hath a trade hath an estate, and he that hath a calling hath an office of profit and honor; but then the trade must be worked at, and the calling well followed, or neither the estate, nor the office, will enable us to pay our taxes."

"If we are industrious we shall never starve; for, as Poor Richard says, at the working man's house hunger looks in, but dares not enter.

Nor will the bailiff nor the constable enter, for industry pays debts, while despair encreaseth them, says Poor Richard.

What though you have found no treasure, nor has any rich relation left you a legacy, <u>diligence is the mother of good luck</u>, as Poor Richard says, and God gives all things to industry.

Then plough deep, while sluggards sleep, and you shall have corn to sell and to keep, says Poor Dick."

"Work while it is called today, for you know not how much you may be hindered tomorrow, which makes Poor Richard say, one today is worth two tomorrows; and farther, have you somewhat to do tomorrow, do it today.

If you were a servant, would you not be ashamed that a good master should catch you idle? Are you then your own master, be ashamed to catch yourself idle, as Poor Dick says.

When there is so much to be done for yourself, your family, your country, and your gracious king, be up by peep of day; let not the sun look down and say, inglorious here he lies. Handle your tools without mittens; remember that the cat in gloves catches no mice, as Poor Richard says."

'Tis true there is much to be done, and perhaps you are weak handed, but stick to it steadily, and you will see great effects, for constant dropping wears away stones, and by diligence and patience the mouse ate in two the cable; and little strokes fell great oaks, as Poor Richard says in his almanac, the year I cannot just now remember. "Methinks I hear some of you say, must a man afford himself no leisure? I will tell thee, my friend, what Poor Richard says, employ thy time well if thou meanest to gain leisure; and, since thou art not sure of a minute, throw not away an hour. Leisure is time for doing something useful; this leisure the diligent man will obtain, but the lazy man never; so that, as Poor Richard says, a life of leisure and a life of laziness are two things. Do you imagine that sloth will afford you more comfort than labor? No, for as Poor Richard says, trouble springs from idleness, and grievous toil from needless ease. Many without labor would live by their wits only, but they break for want of stock.

Whereas industry gives comfort, and plenty, and respect: fly pleasures, and they'll follow you."

"The diligent spinner has a large shift, and now I have a sheep and a cow, everybody bids me good morrow, all which is well said by Poor Richard."

"But with our industry, we must likewise be steady, settled and careful, and oversee our own affairs with our own eyes, and not trust too much to others; for, as Poor Richard says, I never saw an oft removed tree, Nor yet an oft removed family, That throve so well as those that settled be."

"And again, three removes is as bad as a fire, and again, keep the shop, and thy shop will keep thee; and again, if you would have your business done, go; if not, send. And again, He that by the plough would thrive, Himself must either hold or drive."

"And again, the eye of a master will do more work than both his hands; and again, want of care does us more damage than want of knowledge; and again, not to oversee workmen is to leave them your purse open.

Trusting too much to others' care is the ruin of many; for, as the almanac says, in the affairs of this world men are saved not by faith, but by the want of it; but a man's own care is profitable; for, saith Poor

Dick, learning is to the studious, and riches to the careful, as well as power to the bold, and Heaven to the virtuous. And farther, if you would have a faithful servant, and one that you like, serve yourself. And again, he adviseth to circumspection and care, even in the smallest matters, because sometimes a little neglect may breed great mischief; adding, for want of a nail the shoe was lost; for want of a shoe the horse was lost, and for want of a horse the rider was lost, being overtaken and slain by the enemy, all for want of care about a horse-shoe nail."

"So much for industry, my friends, and attention to one's own business; but to these we must add frugality, if we would make our industry more certainly successful.

A man may, if he knows not how to save as he gets, keep his nose all his life to the grindstone, and die not worth a groat at last.

A fat kitchen makes a lean will, as Poor Richard says; and, Many estates are spent in the getting. Since women for tea forsook spinning and knitting, and men for punch forsook hewing and splitting. If you would be wealthy, says he, in another almanac, think of saving as well as of getting:

the Indies have not made Spain rich, because her outgoes are greater than her incomes.

Away then with your expensive follies, and you will not have so much cause to complain of hard times, heavy taxes, and chargeable families; for, as Poor Dick says, Women and wine, game and deceit, Make the wealth small, and the wants great. And farther, what maintains one vice, would bring up two children. You may think perhaps that a little tea, or a little punch now and then, diet a little more costly, clothes a little finer, and a little entertainment now and then, can be no great Matter; but remember what Poor Richard says, many a little makes a mickle, and farther, beware of little expenses; a small leak will sink a great ship, and again, who dainties love, shall beggars prove, and moreover, fools make Feasts, and wise men eat them."

"Here you are all got together at this vendue of fineries and knicknacks. You call them goods, but if you do not take care, they will prove evils to some of you.

You expect they will be sold cheap, and perhaps they may for less than they cost; but if you have no occasion for them, they must be dear to you.

Remember what Poor Richard says, buy what thou hast no need of, and ere long thou shalt sell thy necessaries. And again, at a great pennyworth pause a while: he means, that perhaps the cheapness is apparent only, and not real;

or the bargain, by straining thee in thy business, may do thee more harm than good. For in another place he says, many have been ruined by buying good pennyworths."

Again, Poor Richard says,

'tis foolish to lay our money in a purchase of repentance; and yet this folly is practised every day at vendues, for want of minding the almanac.'

"Wise men, as Poor Dick says, learn by others' harms, fools scarcely by their own, but, felix quem faciunt aliena pericula cautum.

Many a one, for the sake of finery on the back, have gone with a hungry belly, and half-starved their families; silks and satins, scarlet and velvets, as Poor Richard says, put out the kitchen fire. These are not the necessaries of life; they can scarcely be called the conveniencies, and yet only because they look pretty, how many want to have them.

The artificial wants of mankind thus become more numerous than the natural; and, as Poor Dick says, for one poor person, there are an hundred indigent.

By these, and other extravagancies, the genteel are reduced to poverty, and forced to borrow of those whom they formerly despised, but who through industry and frugality have maintained their standing; in which case it appears plainly, that a ploughman on his legs is higher than a gentleman on his knees, as Poor Richard says. Perhaps they have had a small estate left them, which they knew not the getting of; they think 'tis day, and will never be night; that a little to be spent out of so much, is not worth minding; (a child and a fool, as Poor Richard says, imagine twenty shillings and twenty years can never be spent) but, always taking out of the meal-tub, and never putting in, soon comes to the bottom; then, as Poor Dick says, when the well's dry, they know the worth of water."

But this they might have known before, if they had taken his advice;

"if you would know the value of money, go and try to borrow some, for, he that goes a borrowing goes a sorrowing, and indeed so does he that lends to such people, when he goes to get it in again."

Poor Dick farther advises, and says, Fond pride of dress, is sure a very curse;

"E'er fancy you consult, consult your purse. And again, pride is as loud a beggar as want, and a great deal more saucy.

When you have bought one fine thing you must buy ten more, that your appearance maybe all of a piece; but Poor Dick says, 'tis easier to suppress the first desire than to satisfy all that follow it.

And 'tis as truly folly for the poor to ape the rich, as for the frog to swell, in order to equal the ox."

"Great estates may venture more, But little boats should keep near shore.

'Tis however a folly soon punished; for pride that dines on vanity sups on contempt,' as Poor Richard says.

And in another place, pride breakfasted with plenty, dined with poverty, and supped with infamy. And after all, of what use is this pride of appearance, for which so much is risked, so much is suffered?

It cannot promote health; or ease pain; it makes no increase of merit in the person, it creates envy, it hastens misfortune.

What is a butterfly? At best He's but a caterpillar dressed. The gaudy fop's his picture just, as Poor Richard says."

"But what madness must it be to run in debt for these superfluities!

We are offered, by the terms of this vendue, six months' credit; and that perhaps has induced some of us to attend it, because we cannot spare the ready money, and hope now to be fine without it. But, ah, think what you do when you run in debt; you give to another power over your liberty.

If you cannot pay at the time, you will be ashamed to see your creditor; you will be in fear when you speak to him, you will make poor pitiful sneaking excuses, and by degrees come to lose you veracity, and sink into base downright lying; for, as Poor Richard says, the second vice is lying, the first is running in debt. And again to the same purpose, lying rides upon debt's back."

"Whereas a freeborn Englishman ought not to be ashamed or afraid to see or speak to any man living. But poverty often deprives a man of all spirit and virtue: 'tis hard for an empty bag to stand upright, as Poor Richard truly says.

What would you think of that Prince, or that government, who should issue an edict forbidding you to dress like a gentleman or a gentlewoman, on pain of imprisonment or servitude?

Would you not say, that you are free, have a right to dress as you please, and that such an edict would be a breach of your privileges, and such a government tyrannical?

And yet you are about to put yourself under that tyranny when you run in debt for such dress!

Your creditor has authority at his pleasure to deprive you of your liberty, by confining you in gaol for life, or to sell you for a servant, if you should not be able to pay him!

When you have got your bargain, you may, perhaps, think little of payment; but creditors, Poor Richard tells us, have better memories than debtors, and in another place says, creditors are a superstitious sect, great observers of set days and times.

The day comes round before you are aware, and the demand is made before you are prepared to satisfy it. Or if you bear your debt in mind, the term which at first seemed so long, will, as it lessens, appear extremely short.

Time will seem to have added wings to his heels as well as shoulders.

Those have a short Lent, saith Poor Richard, who owe money to be paid at Easter."

"Then since, as he says, the borrower is a slave to the lender, and the debtor to the creditor, disdain the chain, preserve your freedom; and maintain your independency: be industrious and free; be frugal and free.

At present, perhaps, you may think yourself in thriving circumstances, and that you can bear a little extravagance without injury; but, For age and want, save while you may; No morning sun lasts a whole day, as Poor Richard says.

Gain may be temporary and uncertain, but ever while you live, expense is constant and certain; and 'tis easier to build two chimneys than to keep one in fuel, as Poor Richard says.

So rather go to bed supperless than rise in debt. Get what you can, and what you get hold; 'Tis the stone that will turn all your lead into gold, as Poor Richard says.

And when you have got the philosopher's stone, sure you will no longer complain of bad times, or the difficulty of paying taxes."

"This doctrine, my friends, is reason and wisdom; but after all, do not depend too much upon your own industry, and frugality, and prudence, though excellent things, for they may all be blasted without the blessing of heaven; and therefore ask that blessing humbly, and be not uncharitable to those that at present seem to want it, but comfort and help them.

Remember Job suffered, and was afterwards prosperous."

"And now to conclude, experience keeps a dear school, but fools will learn in no other, and scarce in that, for it is true, we may give advice, but we cannot give conduct, as Poor Richard says: however, remember this, they that won't be counseled, can't be helped, as Poor Richard says: and farther, that if you will not hear reason, she'll surely rap your knuckles."

Thus the old gentleman ended his harangue.

The people heard it, and approved the doctrine, and immediately practiced the contrary, just as if it had been a common sermon; for the vendue opened, and they began to buy extravagantly, notwithstanding all his cautions, and their own fear of taxes.

I found the good man had thoroughly studied my almanacs, and digested all I had dropped on those topics during the course of five-and-twenty years.

The frequent mention he made of me must have tired anyone else, but my vanity was wonderfully delighted with it, though I was conscious that not a tenth part of the wisdom was my own which he ascribed to me, but rather the gleanings I had made of the sense of all ages and nations.

However, I resolved to be the better for the echo of it; and though I had at first determined to buy stuff for a new coat, I went away resolved to wear my old one a little longer.

Reader, if thou wilt do the same, thy profit will be as great as mine. I am, as ever, thine to serve thee.

If

by Rudyard Kipling

If you can keep your head when all about you
Are losing theirs and blaming it on you,
If you can trust yourself when all men doubt you,
But make allowance for their doubting too;
If you can wait and not be tired by waiting,
Or being lied about, don't deal in lies,
Or being hated, don't give way to hating,
And yet don't look too good, nor talk too wise:

If you can dream—and not make dreams your master;
If you can think—and not make thoughts your aim;
If you can meet with Triumph and Disaster
And treat those two impostors just the same;
If you can bear to hear the truth you've spoken
Twisted by knaves to make a trap for fools,
Or watch the things you gave your life to, broken,
And stoop and build 'em up with worn-out tools:

If you can make one heap of all your winnings
And risk it on one turn of pitch-and-toss,
And lose, and start again at your beginnings
And never breathe a word about your loss;
If you can force your heart and nerve and sinew
To serve your turn long after they are gone,

And so hold on when there is nothing in you
Except the Will which says to them: 'Hold on!'

If you can talk with crowds and keep your virtue,
Or walk with Kings—nor lose the common touch,
If neither foes nor loving friends can hurt you,
If all men count with you, but none too much;
If you can fill the unforgiving minute
With sixty seconds' worth of distance run,
Yours is the Earth and everything that's in it,
And—which is more—you'll be a Man, my son!

Invictus

by William Earnest Henley

Out of the night that covers me,
Black as the pit from pole to pole,
I thank whatever gods may be
For my unconquerable soul.
In the fell clutch of circumstance
I have not winced nor cried aloud.
Under the bludgeonings of chance
My head is bloody, but unbowed.
Beyond this place of wrath and tears
Looms but the Horror of the shade,
And yet the menace of the years
Finds and shall find me unafraid.
It matters not how strait the gate,
How charged with punishments the scroll,
I am the master of my fate:
I am the captain of my soul.

Finally, the most important quality to which the author, because of his experience, aspires and recommends that others also adopt as a goal follows:

Prayer of St. Francis of Assisi

Lord, make me an instrument of your peace:
Where there is hatred, let me sow love
Where there is doubt, faith
Where there is despair, hope
Where there is darkness, light
Where there is sadness, joy

Divine Master
Grant that I may not so much seek to be consoled as to console
To be understood as to understand
To be loved as to love

For it is in giving that we receive
It is in pardoning that we are pardoned
It is in dying that we are born to eternal life.

Amen.

About the Author

The author of this treatise has spent a lifetime developing recognition capabilities and engaging the challenges of leadership teaching inexperienced, ineffective, but motivated, individuals to become effective leaders. This book is an attempt to communicate the relevant knowledge that he has accumulated.

The author's experience is unusually varied and typically at a high decision-making level. It covers politics where he was a delegate to a national presidential nominating convention and served as a planning commissioner for a major American city.

He has been a principal in industrial ventures such as mining, where he secured the rights to a mine that had produced more than six thousand ounces of gold and in which he found new veins of gold. His construction enterprises included building classrooms and multipurpose conference halls for high school districts, and also an animal hospital for a municipal zoo. He has drilled oil wells in Tennessee and experimented with techniques for the recovery of nonproducing older wells.

The experience includes financial products where he founded an insurance agency that developed new approaches to retirement plans. He engaged in small and minority business development pursuant to government contracts. This included providing minority businesses with support services paid for by government programs. He programed a computer accounting system before the development of Quicken and QuickBooks. He has engaged in the successful development of numerous real estate housing, commercial, and industrial projects and has invented methods of financing to develop low-income housing. He served as chairman of the board of a national bank and spent two decades in the practice of law.

He has developed inventions and assisted others in bringing new technologies to market. He has developed procedures and protocols for the installation of portable housing infrastructure products where there are no utilities available. He has also served as a professor of history and chairman of an academic department of a state university. He has engaged in private investment banking, developed real estate syndications, and has authored and published financial securities private placement memorandum documents and offering circulars.

Because of this long and varied, hands-on background in creating new approaches to law, finance, construction and development, insurance, education, and new technologies, the author sees meaning, problems to be solved, and opportunities for good fortune almost everywhere. For him, the key now is focusing on that which is important today and in the future. Part of what is important is sharing his insights and knowledge for the future good. That was the genesis for writing this book.

Rico Vidas
Pasadena, California
September 25, 2019